Financial Technology (FinTech) and Digital Banking in India

Financial Technology (FinTech) and Digital Banking in India

By

Jaspal Singh (IPS)

New Century Publications
New Delhi, India

NEW CENTURY PUBLICATIONS
4852 / 24, 1st Floor,
Ansari Road, Daryaganj,
New Delhi – 110 002 (India)

Tel.: 011-4101 7798; 4358 7398; 98112 66355
E-mail: info@newcenturypublications.com

www.newcenturypublications.com

Editorial office:
4800 / 24, Bharat Ram Road,
Ansari Road, Daryaganj,
New Delhi – 110 002

Reprint: 2024

ISBN: **978-81-7708-538-9**

First Published: 2022

Published by New Century Publications and printed at Milan Enterprises, New Delhi.

Designs: Patch Creative Unit, New Delhi.

PRINTED IN INDIA

About the Book

FinTech is an umbrella term coined in the recent past to denote technological innovations having a bearing on financial services. FinTech is a contraction of the words *finance* and *technology*. It refers to the technological start-ups that are emerging to challenge traditional banking and financial players and covers an array of services, from crowd funding platforms and mobile payment solutions to online portfolio management tools and international money transfers.

Artificial intelligence (AI) refers to the simulation of human intelligence in machines that are programmed to think like humans and mimic their actions. Artificial intelligence (AI) has applications in the financial industry, where it is used to detect and flag activity in banking and finance such as unusual debit card usage and large account deposits.

India has a rich diversity of digital payment options. Many of these are interoperable, and work through bank accounts, thus giving the users a lot more choice. However, the costs of digital payments are still an issue, and acceptance infrastructure is not widespread.

This book explains and examines various aspects of financial technology (FinTech) and digital banking in simple and non-technical language. It contains 17 chapters which have been organized into 2 parts.

Part I (chapters 1 to 3) is titled Financial Technology (FinTech) and Artificial Intelligence (AI). It provides conceptual clarity as regards FinTech and the major FinTech innovations and services. It also explains the basics of AI.

Part II (chapters 4 to 17) is titled Digital Banking in India. It deals with various forms of payment systems, Reserve Bank of India (RBI) and other organizations linked to payment systems, paper-based traditional systems of payment, electronic payments (e-payments), card-based e-payment, non-card e-payment, internet banking, mobile banking, cyber space, cyber attacks and cyber security, and data protection strategies and technologies.

About the Author

Shri Jaspal Singh (IPS) is currently Director General of Police, Goa. He joined the Indian Police Service in 1996 and has served in Delhi, Goa, Puducherry and Andaman and Nicobar (A&N) Islands in various capacities. He has handled field assignments for 12 years in different ranks.

He is the recipient of the Police Medal for Meritorious Service, Police Medal for Hard Duty and Lt. Governor's Commendation for exemplary work in A&N Islands during the massive earthquake and Tsunami.

While still a student, he was nominated as a member of the University Senate by the Governor of Punjab for his excellence in academics.

Shri Jaspal graduated with Honours in Economics from Guru Nanak Dev University (GNDU), Amritsar, Punjab and also completed his LL.M. from University of Delhi, Delhi. He also holds a Post-graduate degree in Management from GNDU, Amritsar, Punjab and a Masters degree in Computer Applications from Indira Gandhi National Open University (IGNOU), New Delhi. He was also a faculty member of the Department of Business Management, GNDU, Amritsar, Punjab. He also served as a senior executive with state-owned Hindustan Petroleum Corporation Limited.

He has received training with the Police Department of Los Angeles (US) and also attended a course organized by the US Department of State on Advanced Explosive Incident Counter Measures.

Shri Jaspal had already authored the book *Digital Payments in India: Background, Trends and Opportunities* (2019) and also compiled a book titled *Aman Ka Gehwara*.

Contents

Preface

The term *FinTech* is a contraction of the words *finance* and *technology*. It refers to the technological start-ups that are emerging to challenge traditional banking and financial players and covers an array of services, from crowd funding platforms and mobile payment solutions to online portfolio management tools and international money transfers. FinTech is an umbrella term coined in the recent past to denote technological innovation having a bearing on financial services.

FinTech is broad term used to describe emerging technological innovations in the financial services sector, with ever increasing reliance on information technology. Starting as a term referring to the backend technology used by large financial institutions, it has expanded to include technological innovation in the financial sector, including innovations in financial literacy and education, retail banking, investments etc.

Artificial intelligence (AI) has applications in the financial industry, where it is used to detect and flag activity in banking and finance such as unusual debit card usage and large account deposits—all of which help fraud department of a bank.

Artificial intelligence (AI) refers to the simulation of human intelligence in machines that are programmed to think like humans and mimic their actions. The term may also be applied to any machine that exhibits traits associated with a human mind such as learning and problem-solving. The ideal characteristic of artificial intelligence is its ability to rationalize and take actions that have the best chance of achieving a specific goal.

Banking system forms the core of the financial sector of an economy. Role of commercial banks is particularly important in underdeveloped countries. Through mobilisation of resources and their better allocation, commercial banks play an important role in the development process of underdeveloped countries. By offering attractive saving schemes and ensuring safety of deposits, commercial banks encourage willingness to save among the people. By reaching out to people in rural areas, they help convert idle savings into effective ones. Commercial banks improve the allocation of resources by lending money to priority sectors of the economy. These banks provide a meeting ground for the savers and the investors.

The banking industry all over the world has undergone transformation since the early 1980s under the impact of deregulation, advances in information technology and globalisation. Banks have traditionally been in the forefront of harnessing technology to improve their products, services and efficiency.

Due to steps taken by the Reserve Bank of India (RBI) to encourage electronic transactions, paper-based systems (cheque, demand draft, banker's cheque, payment order, travellers' cheque, interest warrant, dividend warrants, and money order) constitute a miniscule portion of retail payments. The number of clearing houses has also declined.

India has a rich diversity of digital payment options. Many of these are interoperable, and work through bank accounts, thus giving the users a lot more choice. However, the costs of digital payments are still an issue, and acceptance infrastructure is not widespread.

Card-based electronic payment systems are well-understood at the global and national level, and find acceptance at stores, as well as for online payments. India has had the presence of international players in the payments space for many years. Recently, an Indian player—National Payments Corporation of India (NPCI)—has also introduced card payments through the RuPay scheme.

Cards are usually issued by banks and can be classified on the basis of their issuance, usage and payment by the card holder. There are three types of cards: (a) pre-paid cards, (b) debit cards and (c) credit cards.

In recent years, non-card electronic payment systems have become very popular. Advancements in banking technology, progress in mobile banking and innovative technologies to facilitate digital payments have enabled large number of small denomination transactions to be handled smoothly in electronic mode. The Government of India has taken policy decisions to encourage cashless/electronic transactions.

Cyber space is a complex environment consisting of interactions among people, software services, devices, networks and worldwide distribution of information and communication technology (ICT).

Owing to the numerous benefits brought about by technological advancements, the cyber space is a common pool used by citizens, businesses, critical information infrastructure, military and governments in a manner that makes it difficult to draw clear boundaries among these different groups. The cyber space is expected to be more complex in the foreseeable future, with many-fold increase in networks and devices connected to it.

One of the biggest attractions of cyber space, as an electronic medium, is its openness and freedom. It is a public domain and there is no restriction on who can use it as long as one adheres to its technical parameters. This has also given rise to concerns over the security of data and information and privacy.

Cyber space is vulnerable to a wide variety of incidents, whether intentional or accidental, man-made or natural, and the data exchanged in the cyber space can be exploited for nefarious purposes by both nation-states and non-state actors.

Cyber attacks and threats are faced by individuals, businesses and governments. These can take the following forms: (a) phishing, (b) hacking, (c) scamming, (d) sniffing, (e) spoofing and (f) denial of service attack.

The only way to protect ourselves from such activities is to be vigilant about our data and protect the data from getting into the hands of scamsters and fraudsters.

Consequences of cyber attacks are disastrous. Large-scale cyber incidents may overwhelm the government, public and private sector resources and services by disrupting functioning of critical information systems. Complications from disruption of such a magnitude may threaten lives, economy and national security.

Openness and freedom of use of the cyber space has given rise to concerns over the security of data and information and privacy. These concerns are common to any network including closed user group networks. However, over the internet, the dimensions of risk are larger while the control measures are relatively fewer.

Rapid identification, information exchange, investigation and co-ordinated response and remediation can mitigate the damage caused by malicious cyber space activity.

To improve customer confidence in digital payments, it is of utmost importance to keep a control on the number of frauds that occur, and to ensure that customers are not impacted.

Acknowledgements

This work draws, in part, on the information provided in the publications and websites of various national and international institutions/organizations, in particular the Ministry of Finance, Government of India, Ministry of Communications, Government of India, Ministry of Electronics and Information Technology, Government of India, Reserve Bank of India (RBI), National Payments Corporation of India (NPCI), and NITI Aayog. Use of information from these sources is gratefully acknowledged.

Goa **Jaspal Singh**

July 2022

Explanation of Select Terms Used in the Book

Aadhaar Payment Bridge System (APBS): It is a unique payment system implemented by National Payments Corporation of India (NPCI), which uses Aadhaar number as a central key for electronically channelizing government subsidies and benefits in the Aadhaar-enabled bank accounts (AEBA) of the intended beneficiaries. It is a payment system based on Aadhaar numbers issued by UIDAI and issuer identification number (IIN)) issued by NPCI. APBS is used by the government departments and agencies for the transfer of benefits and subsidies under Direct Benefit Transfer (DBT) scheme launched by Government of India.

Aadhaar-enabled Payment System (AEPS): AEPS is a payment service offered by the National Payments Corporation of India (NPCI) to banks, financial institutions using Aadhaar. AEPS is a bank-led model, which allows online financial inclusion transaction at micro ATM through the business correspondent (BC) of any bank using the Aadhaar authentication. This system is designed to handle both ON-US (intra-bank) and OFF-US (inter-bank) requests seamlessly in an effective way by enabling authentication gateway for all Aadhaar-linked account holders.

Artificial Intelligence (AI): AI refers to the simulation of human intelligence in machines that are programmed to think like humans and mimic their actions. The term may also be applied to any machine that exhibits traits associated with a human mind such as learning and problem-solving. The ideal characteristic of artificial intelligence is its ability to rationalize and take actions that have the best chance of achieving a specific goal.

Banker's Cheque: It is an instrument used by banks to settle payment obligations on behalf of their customers. Bankers's cheque is guaranteed by the bank for its full value and is similar to a demand draft. In fact, these instruments are payable at the branch of issue and used for making payment within the local clearing jurisdiction.

Bharat Interface for Money (BHIM): BHIM is a national system for account-to-account transfers. It is a one app for all users from all banks. It ensures direct transactions from and to your bank account. It is a mobile app developed by NPCI based on the unified payment interface (UPI).

Biometrics: It involves identification and verification of an individual based on some physical characteristic, such as fingerprint analysis, hand geometry, or retina scanning. This technology is advancing rapidly, and offers an alternative means to authenticate a user.

Blockchain Technology: Blockchain is a distributed ledger in which transactions—e.g. involving digital currencies or securities—are stored as blocks (groups of transactions that are performed around the same point in time) on computers that are connected to the network. The ledger grows as the chain of blocks increases in size. Each new block of transactions has to be verified by the network before it can be added to the chain. This means that each computer connected to the network has full information about the transactions in the network.

Cloud Computing: Cloud-based IT services can deliver internet-based access to a shared pool of computing resources that can be quickly and easily deployed. Infrastructure, platform service and mobile back-end as a service are offered under cloud-based services. The use of these services is an important enabler for new entrants to the financial services arena to set up quickly and with low start-up cost; with easy options to expand their capability as the firm grows.

Credit Cards: A credit card is a payment card issued to users (cardholders) to enable the cardholder to pay a merchant for goods and services, based on the cardholder's promise to the card issuer to pay them for the amounts so paid plus other agreed charges. The card issuer (usually a bank) creates a revolving account and grants a line of credit to the cardholder, from which the cardholder can borrow money for payment to a merchant or as a cash advance.

Crowd Funding: Crowd funding is a way of raising debt or equity from multiple investors via internet-based platform. Securities and Exchange Board of India (SEBI) has defined crowd funding as “solicitation of funds (small amount) from multiple investors through a web-based platform or social networking site for a specific project, business venture or social cause”.

Cryptography: The process of disguising a message in such a way as to hide its substance is called encryption. An encrypted message is called cipher text. The process of turning a cipher text back into plain text is called decryption. Cryptography is the art and science of keeping messages secure. It uses a *key* for encrypting or decrypting a message. Both the method of encryption and the size of key are important to ensure confidentiality of a message.

Cyber Space: Cyber space is a complex environment consisting of interactions among people, software services, devices, networks and worldwide distribution of information and communication technology. One of the biggest attractions of cyber space, as an electronic medium, is its openness and freedom. It is a public domain and there is no restriction on who can use it as long as one adheres to its technical parameters. This has also given rise to concerns over the security of data and information and privacy.

Data Protection: Data protection is the process of safeguarding important information from corruption, compromise or loss. The importance of data protection increases as the amount of data created and stored continues to grow at unprecedented rates.

Debit Cards: A debit card is a plastic payment card that can be used instead of cash when making purchases. Debit card is issued by the bank where a client has an account. Linked to the bank account, debit cards are issued to account holders and any expenditure made is immediately debited to user's account. User can use this card to withdraw cash up to the limit prescribed by the bank.

Demand Draft: It is a pre-paid negotiable instrument stating that the drawee bank undertakes to make payment in full when the instrument is presented by the payee for payment. It is payable on a specified branch of a bank at a specified centre. To receive payment, the beneficiary has to either present the instrument directly to the bank branch concerned or to get it collected though his/her bank by the clearing mechanism.

Denial of Service Attack: It represents an attempt to overwhelm a server with requests so that it cannot respond to legitimate traffic. A denial of service attack typically bombards websites with requests, overloading the portal until its server crashes, thus denying access of the website to legitimate users. Such attacks reduce internet speed to almost zero.

Digital Currencies (DCs): DCs are digital representations of value, currently issued by private developers and denominated in their own unit of account. They are obtained, stored, accessed, and transacted electronically and neither denominated in any sovereign currency nor issued or backed by any government or central bank.

Digital Economy: It refers to an economy that is based on digital technologies. The digital economy is also sometimes called the *internet economy*, *new economy*, or *web economy*. Increasingly, the *digital economy* is intertwined with the traditional economy making a clear delineation harder. In this new economy, digital networking and communication infrastructures provide a global platform over which people and organizations devise strategies, interact, communicate, collaborate and search for information.

Digital Forensics: Digital forensic is a branch of forensic science encompassing the recovery and investigation of material found in digital devices, often in relation to computer crime. The term digital forensics was originally used as a synonym for computer forensics but has expanded to cover investigation of all devices capable of storing digital data.

Digital Payment: According to RBI's Ombudsman Scheme for digital transactions, "*digital transaction* means a payment transaction in a seamless system effected without the need for cash at least in one of the two legs, if not in both. This includes transactions made through digital/electronic modes wherein both the originator and the beneficiary use digital/electronic medium to send or receive money".

Digital Wallet or Electronic Wallet (E-Wallet): Digital wallet is essentially digital versions of traditional wallet that someone would carry in his pocket. It is a type of electronic card which is used for transactions made online through a computer or a smart phone. The utility of digital wallet is the same as that of a credit or debit card. A digital wallet needs to be linked with the individual's bank account to make payments.

Digitization: Digitization is the process by which technology lowers the costs of storing, sharing, and analyzing data. This process has changed how financial institutions behave, how industrial activities are organized, and how governments operate.

Distributed Ledgers Technology (DLT): DLT provides complete and secure transaction records, updated and verified by users, removing the need for a central authority. These technologies allow for direct peer-to-peer transactions, which might offer benefits, in terms of efficiency and security, over existing technological solutions.

E-aggregators: E-aggregators provide internet-based venues for retail customers to compare the prices and features of a range of financial (and non-financial) products such as standardised insurance, mortgages, and deposit account products. They can also be firms that provide services that allow users to aggregate and analyse their data on their payment patterns, across separate accounts and products (e.g. Yodlee). E-aggregators also provide an easy way to switch between providers and may become a major distributor for a variety of financial products.

Electronic Banking (E-banking): It is a generic term encompassing internet banking, telephone banking, mobile banking etc. In other words, it is a process of delivery of banking services and products through electronic channels such as satellite, telephone, internet, cell phone etc.

E-payments: E-payments are defined as the exchange or transfer of funds over an electronic payment system. Payments through these electronic platforms can be made by various means, including but not limited to payment card, e-wallet, direct deposit, direct debit, electronic funds transfer and wire transfer. The payment component is only one part of the e-payments process, which can also include online submission of forms and the provision of online instructions or calculators to facilitate the use of an e-payments system.

e-Rupi: It is a digital payment solution launched in August 2021. It is a person-specific, and purpose-specific digital voucher where it is not required for the customer to have a bank account and is operable on basic phones, even in areas which lack an internet connection.

Financial Technology (FinTech): The term FinTech is a contraction of the words *finance* and *technology*. It refers to the technological start-ups that are emerging to challenge traditional banking and financial players and covers an array of services, from crowd funding platforms and mobile payment solutions to online portfolio management tools and international money transfers.

Firewalls: Firewalls are a component or set of components that restrict access between a protected network and the outside world (i.e., the internet). They control traffic between outside and inside a network, providing a single entry point where access control and auditing can be imposed. All firewalls examine the pieces or packets of data flowing into and out of a network and determine whether a particular person should be given access inside the network. As a result, unauthorized computers outside the firewall are prevented from directly accessing the computers inside the internal network.

Hacking: It refers to the practice of breaking into a computer without authorisation, for malicious reasons, just to prove it can be done, or for other personal reasons.

Immediate Payment Services (IMPS): IMPS is a real-time fund transfer platform available 24x7x365. On October 8, 2021, RBI increased the daily limit of IMPS transactions from ₹ 2 lakh to ₹ 5 lakh which should further help in boosting digital payments. It is a non-card retail payment service operated by National Payments Corporation of India (NPCI) in collaboration with member banks.

National Automated Clearing House (NACH): NACH is meant for banks, financial institutions, corporates and government. It is a web-based solution to facilitate inter-bank, high volume, electronic transactions which are repetitive and periodic in nature.

National Electronic Funds Transfer (NEFT): NEFT is an electronic message-based payment system, and was introduced by the RBI in November 2005. NEFT is a nation-wide payments system facilitating one-to-one fund transfer up to ₹ 2 lakh, usually on the same day. NEFT is more secure, nation-wide retail electronic payment system to facilitate funds transfer by the bank customers, between the networked bank branches in the country. This has facilitated the availability of electronic payment modes at more centres.

National Electronic Toll Collection (NETC) System: It facilitates an automated and interoperable electronic toll collection structure across the country's network of highways. NETC operates under the brand name Fastag, and it allows tolls to be collected digitally on national highways, allowing smoother movement of vehicles. NETC operates through a linked closed loop wallet, which is funded by the user. Only bank issuers, and acquirers are permitted to operate under NETC.

Peer-to-peer (P2P) Lending: P2P lenders connect lenders and borrowers, using advanced technologies to speed up loan acceptance. These technologies are designed to increase the efficiency and reduce the time involved in access to credit. While P2P lending originally involved direct matching of individual lenders and borrowers on a one-to-one basis, it has evolved into a form of market place lending where institutional and high net worth individual investors lend into a pool that borrowers can access.

Phishing: It is the fraudulent practice of sending e-mails purporting to be from reputable companies in order to induce individuals to reveal personal information, such as passwords and credit card numbers.

Point-of-Sale (PoS) Terminals: Point-of-sale commonly known as *checkout* is the location where transaction occurs for the sale of goods or services and customers can pay for their purchases. It is an alternative for an electronic cash register and is referred as PoS terminal, which is nothing but a combination of both the hardware and software used for the checkouts. PoS hardware is equipment for PoS system, which includes card-reading machines, printers, cash registers and computer systems.

Pre-paid Cards: These are pre-loaded from a customer's bank account and are equivalent to cash. These can be used for limited amount of transaction and can be recharged several times like mobile recharge. Such cards are safe to use. Pre-paid instruments are payment instruments that facilitate purchase of goods and services against the value stored on these instruments.

Real Time Gross Settlement (RTGS): RTGS is a funds transfer systems where transfer of money takes place from one bank to another on a *real time* and on *gross* basis. Settlement in *real time* means payment transaction is not subjected to any waiting period. *Gross settlement* means the transaction is settled on one-to-one basis without bunching or netting with any other transaction. Once processed, payments are final and irrevocable.

RuPay: RuPay is an Indian domestic card payment scheme conceived and launched by National Payments Corporation of India (NPCI). It aims to fulfil RBI's vision to offer a domestic, open-loop, multilateral system which will allow all Indian banks and financial institutions in India to participate in electronic payments. RuPay, the word itself has a sense of nationality in it. RuPay is the coinage of two terms Rupee and payment.

Scamming: It means creating a fraudulent scheme to dupe innocent people. This has become very common and every day one hears more stories of and people getting duped of massive amounts of money.

Smart Cards: These resemble credit cards or other traditional magnetic stripe cards, but contain an embedded computer chip. The chip includes a processor, operating system, and both read only memory (ROM) and random-access memory (RAM). They can be used to generate one-time passwords when prompted by a host computer, or to carry cryptographic keys. A smart card reader is required for their use.

Smart Contracts: Smart contracts are computer protocols that can self-execute, self-enforce, self-verify, and self-constrain the performance of a contract. Development of smart contracts in relation to financial services could have a large impact on the structure of trade finance or derivatives trading, especially more bespoke contracts, and could also be integrated into Robo-advice wealth management services. The widespread adoption of smart contracts in financial services could be facilitated by the establishment of distributed ledger technology.

Sniffing: It involves the use of a software program that is illicitly inserted somewhere on a network to capture ("sniff") user passwords as they pass through the system.

Spoofing: It refers to an attempt to gain access to a system by posing as an authorised user.

Token Technology: It relies on a separate physical device, which is retained by an individual, to verify the user's identity. The token resembles a small hand-held card or calculator and is used to generate passwords. The device is usually synchronized with security software in the host computer such as an internal clock or an identical time-based mathematical algorithm. Tokens are well suited for one-time password generation and access control. A separate PIN is typically required to activate the token.

Unified Payments Interface (UPI): UPI is a system that powers multiple bank accounts into a single mobile application (of any participating bank), merging several banking features, seamless fund routing and merchant payments into one hood. It is a system for instant electronic payment through user's smart phone. It is an advanced version of immediate payment service (IMPS) which is used to transfer money between bank accounts. Like IMPS, UPI facilitates round-the-clock funds transfer service. It authenticates the identity of the user like a debit card, using the phone as a tool instead of a separate card. It works 24x7 and for 365 days.

Unstructured Supplementary Service Data (USSD): It is a service which aims to take banking services to every layman in the country. This service allows every customer to access banking services with a single number irrespective of the telecom service provider, make of the mobile handset or the region. The service is offered through a National Unified USSD Platform (NUUP) on a short code *99#. The service can be used for payments up to ₹ 5,000 per day per customer.

Abbreviations/Acronyms Used in the Book

ABRS	Aadhaar-based Remittance Service
AEBA	Aadhaar-enabled Bank Accounts
AI	Artificial Intelligence
APB	Aadhaar Payment Bridge
ATMs	Automated Teller Machines
B2G	Business-to-Government
BCs	Business Correspondents
BHIM	Bharat Interface for Money
BIS	Bank for International Settlements
BPSS	Board for Regulation and Supervision of Payment and Settlement Systems
C2G	Citizen-to-Government
CA	Certification Authority
CBLO	Collateralised Borrowing and Lending Obligation
CCIL	Clearing Corporation of India Limited
CCPs	Central Counterparties
CDP	Customer Data Protection
CLS	Continuous-linked Settlement
CNP	Card Not Present
CSCs	Common Service Centres
CTS	Cheque Truncation System
DBT	Direct Benefit Transfer
DCs	Digital Currencies
DES	Data Encryption Standard
DIDS	Distributed Intrusion Detection Systems
DLT	Distributed Ledgers Technology
DMS	Dispute Management System
DoS	Denial-of-Service
DPSS	Department of Payments and Settlement Systems
DvP	Delivery versus Payment
E-banking	Electronic Banking
ECCS	Express Cheque Clearing System

ECS	Electronic Clearing Service
EIU	Economist Intelligence Unit
EU	European Union
E-Wallet	Electronic Wallet
FEMA	Foreign Exchange Management Act
FinTech	Financial Technology
FMIs	Financial Market Infrastructures
FSB	Financial Stability Board
G2B	Government-to-Business
GDPR	General Data Protection Regulation
GEAR	Government E-Payments Adoption Ranking
HR	Human Resources
HVCCS	High Value Cheque Clearing System
IBA	Indian Banks Association
ICOs	Initial Coin Offerings
ICT	Information and Communication Technology
IDBI	Industrial Development Bank of India
IDEA	International Data Encryption Algorithm
IDRBT	Institute for Development and Research in Banking Technology
IDS	Intrusion Detection Systems
IIN	Issuer Identification Number
IMD	International Institute for Management Development
IMF	International Monetary Fund
IMPS	Immediate Payment Service
IOBs	Internet-Only-Banks
IT	Information Technology
IT Act	Information Technology Act
LIC	Life Insurance Corporation of India
MeitY	Ministry of Electronics and Information Technology
MFIs	Micro Finance Institutions
MITCs	Most Important Terms and Conditions
MMID	Mobile Money Identifier
MMS	Mandate Management System

MNOs	Mobile Network Operators
MPIN	Mobile Personal Identification Number
NACH	National Automated Clearing House
NBFCs	Non-banking Financial Companies
NCR	National Capital Region
NCSP	National Cyber Security Policy
NEAT	National Stock Exchange for Automated Trading
NEFT	National Electronic Funds Transfer
NETC	National Electronic Toll Collection
NFC	Near Field Communication
NFS	National Financial Switch
NI Act	Negotiable Instruments Act
NIDS	Network-based Intrusion Detection Systems
NPCI	National Payments Corporation of India
NSCCL	National Securities Clearing Corporation Ltd
P2P	Peer-to-peer
PAN	Permanent Account Number
PCs	Personal Computers
PDO	Public Debt Office
PIN	Personal Identification Number
PKI	Public Key Infrastructure
PoS	Point-of-Sale
PPIs	Pre-paid Payment Instruments
PPP	Public-Private-Partnership
PSS Act	Payment and Settlement Systems Act
R&D	Research and Development
RA	Registration Authority
RAM	Random-Access Memory
RBI	Reserve Bank of India
ROM	Read Only Memory
RTGS	Real Time Gross Settlement System
SBI	State Bank of India
SEBI	Securities and Exchange Board of India
SGL	Subsidiary General Ledger
SHGs	Self-help Groups

SIPI	Systemically Important Payment Infrastructure
SSL	Secure Socket Layer
TRAI	Telecom Regulatory Authority of India
TSR	Total Solution Release
UIDAI	Unique Identification Authority of India
UPI	Unified Payments Interface
URR	Uniform Regulations and Rules
USSD	Unstructured Supplementary Service Data
VAT	Value Added Tax
VLE	Village Level Entrepreneur
VPA	Virtual Payment Address
WAP	Wireless Application Protocol
WLAs	White Label ATMs
WWW	World Wide Web

Part I
Financial Technology (FinTech) and Artificial Intelligence (AI)

1

Financial Technology (FinTech): An Introduction

Information technology (IT) is considered to be one of the most influential developments affecting the global financial sector in the near future. Innovations related to payments, lending, asset management and insurance pose a challenge to business models and strategies of financial institutions. However, these also bring opportunities for both the incumbent market participants and newcomers. Also, innovation can create new risks for individual financial institutions, consumers of financial services, as well as the financial system as a whole. FinTech (also called digital innovations) have emerged as a potentially transformative force in the financial markets.

A couple of decades ago, people had to visit a bank or financial company to apply for a mortgage, small business loan or simply transfer funds from one bank to another. Today, fintech has made it possible to invest, borrow, save and transfer funds through online and mobile services without ever stepping foot inside a bank. Though traditional institutions were slow to adopt fintech solutions, both start-ups and established companies are betting on digitized financial services.

1.1 What is FinTech?

The term *FinTech* is a contraction of the words *finance* and *technology*. It refers to the technological start-ups that are emerging to challenge traditional banking and financial players and covers an array of services, from crowd funding platforms and mobile payment solutions to online portfolio management tools and international money transfers. FinTech is an umbrella term coined in the recent past to denote technological innovation having a bearing on financial services. FinTech is a broad term that requires definition and currently regulators are working on bringing out a common definition.

According to Financial Stability Board (FSB), of the Bank for International Settlements (BIS), "FinTech is technologically enabled financial innovation that could result in new business models, applications, processes, or products with an associated material effect on financial markets and institutions and the provision of financial services". This definition aims at encompassing the wide variety of innovations in financial services enabled by technologies, regardless the type, size and regulatory status of the innovative firm. The broadness of the FSB definition is useful when assessing and anticipating the rapid development of the financial system and financial institutions, and the associated risks and opportunities.

FinTech is broad term used to describe emerging technological innovations in the financial services sector, with ever increasing reliance on information technology. Starting as a term referring to the back end technology used by large financial institutions, it has expanded to include technological innovation in the financial sector, including innovations in financial literacy and education, retail banking, investments etc.

1.2 Evolution of FinTech

Fintech has been around much longer than most people think. While the latest iteration of fintech allows you to pay for a cup of coffee with a mobile app, the history of financial technology can be traced back to the earliest credit cards that were adopted into the general public in the late 1950s. Credit cards generally represent the first fintech products available to the public, in that they eliminated the need for consumers to carry physical currency in their day-to-day lives. From there, fintech evolved to include bank mainframes and online stock trading services. In 1998, PayPal was founded, representing one of the first fintech companies to operate primarily on the internet—a breakthrough that has been further revolutionized by mobile technology, social media, and data encryption. This fintech revolution has led to the mobile payment apps, blockchain networks, and social media-housed payment options we regularly use today.

After the credit card, financial technology evolved and introduced several major milestones to the mass market, such as ATMs, electronic stock exchanges, bank mainframe computers, and online stock exchanges. Each new piece of technology advanced the financial infrastructure that most people used everyday, but rarely had to think about.

Presently, fintech solutions are challenging the traditional financial infrastructure, as more services transition to a new technological paradigm, such as using a payment app on a mobile wallet instead of carrying physical credit cards in a physical wallet. Fintech has revolutionized many different markets, most notably the banking, trading, insurance and risk management industries. Fintech companies, which include start-ups, technology companies and established financial institutions, utilize emerging technologies, such as big data, artificial intelligence, blockchain and edge computing to make financial services more accessible and more efficient.

1.3 Scope of FinTech

Financial services, including banking services, are at the threshold of a revolutionary change driven by technological and digital innovations. A rapidly growing number of financial entities and technology firms are experimenting with technological and financial solutions which either modify the way financial intermediation takes place or leads to disintermediation. FinTech innovations have the potential to deliver a range of benefits, in particular efficiency improvements and cost reductions. Technological developments are also fundamentally changing the way people access financial services and increasing financial inclusion.

Financial innovations (like derivatives) have become a focal point for a lot of attention, and some jurisdictions have decided to take a more active approach in facilitating this innovation. For this purpose, they have taken a variety of regulatory and supervisory initiatives such as regulatory sandboxes, innovation hubs, innovation incubators or accelerators etc.

Technological start-ups are emerging to challenge traditional banking. Some of the major FinTech products and services currently used in the market place are peer to peer (P2P) lending platforms, crowd funding, block chain technology, distributed ledgers technology etc. These FinTech products are currently used in international finance, which bring together the lenders and borrowers, seekers and providers of information, with or without a nodal intermediation agency.

FinTechs are becoming popular both with the users of banking services and investment funds, which see them as the future of the financial sector. Even retail groups and telecom operators are looking for ways to offer financial services via their existing networks. This upsurge of activities raises questions over what kind of financial landscape will emerge in the wake of the digital transformation. Financial institutions and markets are seeking to increase their knowledge in relation to technological innovation, both through partnerships with tech companies and by investing in or acquiring such companies. Nonetheless, there are wide differences in the preparedness of market participants for these changes in practice.

Some of the major FinTech products and services currently used in the market place are peer to peer (P2P) lending platforms, crowd funding, block chain technology, distributed ledgers technology, big data, smart contracts, robo advisors, e-aggregators, etc. These FinTech products are currently used in international finance, which bring together the lenders and borrowers, seekers and providers of information, with or without a nodal intermediation agency.

FinTechs are attracting interest both from users of banking services and investment funds, which see them as the future of the financial sector. Even retail groups and telecom operators are looking for ways to offer financial services via their existing networks. This flurry of activities raises questions over what kind of financial landscape will emerge in the wake of the digital transformation.

1.4 Working Group on FinTech and Digital Banking

Reserve Bank of India (RBI) had set up an inter-regulatory Working Group in July 2016 to study the regulatory issues relating to FinTech and digital banking in India. The Working Group (Chairman: Sudarshan Sen) submitted its report titled *Report of the Working Group on FinTech and Digital Banking* in November 2017. Key recommendations of the Working Group are listed below:

1. There is a need to have a deeper understanding of various FinTech products and their interaction with the financial sector and, thereby, the implications on the financial system, before regulating this space.
2. The regulatory actions may vary from "Disclosure" to "Light-Touch Regulation and Supervision" to a "Tight Regulation and Full-Fledged Supervision", depending on the risk implications.
3. There is a need to develop a more detailed understanding of risks inherent in platform based FinTech.
4. Various financial sector regulators to identify sector specific FinTech products and regulatory approaches.
5. The adoption of digital channels to replace manual time-consuming processes to empower customers and/or workforce in the insurance sector.
6. Innovation labs may be established, including within insurance companies, to combine brand and product managers with technological and analytical resources.
7. As and when any securities market FinTech products are introduced or emerge in the market, regulators may assess the product and see whether it can be monitored by way of registering them as an intermediary or through the activity regulations.
8. Insurance companies may collaborate with "Insurtech" entities or start-ups to provide better customer experience

in a cost effective manner.

9. Financial sector regulators need to engage with FinTech entities in order to chalk out appropriate regulatory response and with a view to re-align regulation and supervision in response to the changing environment.
10. In order to identify and monitor the challenges associated with the development of major FinTech innovations and to assess respond to opportunities and risks arising for the financial system from these innovations, a dedicated organizational structure within each regulator needs to be created.
11. To provide an environment for developing FinTech innovations and testing of applications/APIs developed by banks and FinTech companies.
12. An appropriate framework may be introduced for "Regulatory Sandbox/innovation hub" within a well-defined space and duration where financial sector regulators will provide the requisite regulatory support, so as to increase efficiency, manage risks and create new opportunities for consumers in Indian context similar to other regulatory jurisdictions.
13. In view of unique positioning of IDRBT (Institute for Development and Research in Banking Technology) as a research and development institute, and as indicated by some of its activities, it is felt that IDRBT is well placed to create and maintain a regulatory sandbox in collaboration with RBI for enabling innovators to experiment with their banking solutions for eventual adoption. The Institute may continue to interact with RBI, banks, solution providers regarding testing of new products and services and over a period of time upgrade its infrastructure and skill sets to provide full-fledged regulatory sandbox environment. The Reserve Bank of India may actively engage with the Institute in this regard.
14. Regulatory and legal reforms are essential to enable the sustained development of a digital financial industry for the future.

15. Partnerships among regulators, existing industry players, clients and FinTech firms will enable the development of a more dynamic and robust financial services industry.
16. Regulators may explore the use of Reg Tech that may facilitate the delivery of regulatory requirements more efficiently and effectively than existing capabilities.
17. The organizational structure and human resources (HR) practices of regulators have to be reoriented to meet the challenges of innovation, in terms of adapted HR hiring profiles, learning and educational programmes.
18. There is a need for a stand-alone data protection and privacy law in the country.
19. Models of engagement and checklist to be developed by each regulator for each of the activities.
20. The requirement of increasing the levels of education/ awareness of customers should be highlighted by all market regulators.
21. A self-regulatory body for FinTech companies may be encouraged.

FinTech has significant implications for the entire financial system in India. The multiplicity of firms and a mosaic of business models complicate the classification of the various types of activities, products and transactions covered under the FinTech spectrum.

Though the western world has been using the term FinTech for some time, it has only recently become a buzzword in India. Nevertheless, FinTech has, since quite some time, gathered momentum in the country. However, as of now, the FinTech risks are being looked at more in terms of what is associated with the traditional IT systems, such as cyber security risks. While the IT-related risks are no doubt multiplying manifold under FinTech, the whole gamut of issues under the FinTech umbrella, particularly those of regulatory concern, have to be responded to on priority. It is, therefore, necessary to examine these issues and outline the contours of an appropriate regulatory strategy. However, FinTech treads across several activities that are within the scope of different financial sector regulators.

1.5 Regulation of FinTech

Finance is seen as one of the industries most vulnerable to disruption by software because financial services, much like publishing, are made of information rather than concrete goods. In particular blockchains have the potential to reduce the cost of transacting in a financial system. While finance has been shielded by regulation until now, and weathered the dot-com boom without major upheaval, a new wave of start-ups is increasingly "disaggregating" global banks.

Financial services are among the most heavily regulated sectors in the world. Not surprisingly, regulation has emerged as the number one concern among governments as fintech companies take off. As technology is integrated into financial services processes, regulatory problems for such companies have multiplied. In some instances, the problems are a function of technology. In others, they are a reflection of the tech industry's impatience to disrupt finance.

Regulation is also a problem in the emerging world of crypto currencies. Initial coin offerings (ICOs) are a new form of fundraising that allows start-ups to raise capital directly from lay investors. In most countries, they are unregulated and have become fertile ground for scams and frauds. Regulatory uncertainty for ICOs has also allowed entrepreneurs to slip security tokens disguised as utility tokens past the SEC to avoid fees and compliance costs.

Because of the diversity of offerings in fintech and the disparate industries it touches, it is difficult to formulate a single and comprehensive approach to these problems. For the most part, governments have used existing regulations and, in some cases, customized them to regulate fintech.

In response, the International Monetary Fund (IMF) and the World Bank jointly presented Bali Fintech Agenda on October 11, 2018 which consists of 12 policy elements acting as a guidelines for various governments and central banking institutions to adopt and deploy "rapid advances in financial technology".

Data security is another issue regulators are concerned about because of the threat of hacking as well as the need to protect sensitive consumer and corporate financial data. Leading global fintech companies are proactively turning to cloud technology to meet increasingly stringent compliance regulations.

To sum up, fintech, or financial technology, is the term used to describe any technology that delivers financial services through software, such as online banking, mobile payment apps or even crypto currency. Fintech is a broad category that encompasses many different technologies, but the primary objectives are to change the way consumers and businesses access their finances and compete with traditional financial services.

Up until now, financial services institutions offered a variety of services under a single umbrella. The scope of these services encompassed a broad range from traditional banking activities to mortgage and trading services. In its most basic form, Fintech unbundles these services into individual offerings. The combination of streamlined offerings with technology enables fintech companies to be more efficient and cut down on costs associated with each transaction.

New technologies, like machine learning and artificial intelligence, predictive behavioural analytics, and data-driven marketing, will take the guesswork and habit out of financial decisions. Learning apps will not only learn the habits of users, often hidden to themselves, but will engage users in learning games to make their automatic, unconscious spending and saving decisions better. Fintech is also a keen adaptor of automated customer service technology, utilizing chatbots to and AI interfaces to assist customers with basic task and also keep down staffing costs. Fintech is also being leveraged to fight fraud by leveraging information about payment history to flag transactions that are outside the norm.

2

Major FinTech Innovations and Services

Providers of e-payment services are part of a burgeoning industry now known as fintech—where technology enables financial services—which purports to alter traditional financial business models through the use of modern technology. Fintech firms provide services in digital payments, investments, financing, insurance, advisory services, security and much more. Despite some early worries about inadequate consumer protection from unregulated fintech services, governments are increasingly seizing opportunities to work with fintech firms. A collaborative approach among fintech firms, governments and the traditional financial services industry will serve to mitigate potential drawbacks caused by disruption of the financial industry. Such an approach will also encourage innovation and promote the benefits of fintech like faster provision of financial services, including digital payments adoption. It is no surprise, then, that many emerging-market countries are altering their digital payment growth trajectories thanks to mobile payments.

2.1 Payments, Clearing and Settlement Services

Financial institutions are seeking to increase their knowledge in relation to technological innovation, both through partnerships with tech companies and by investing in or acquiring such companies. Despite this, there are wide differences in the preparedness of market participants for these changes in practice.

Innovations are targeted at improving the speed and efficiency of payments, clearing, and settlement, reducing cost and changing the ways people access financial services and conduct financial transactions. Some of the innovations in areas of payments, clearing and settlements in the financial markets are as follows.

2.1.1 Mobile and Web-based Payment Applications: The majority of developments in the areas of payments are based on mobile technology by providing wrappers over existing payments infrastructure. Examples include Apple Pay, Samsung Pay, and Android Pay, which sit on top of existing card payment infrastructure enabling the user's mobile devices to act as their credit/debit cards. There are also mobile payments built on new payment infrastructure, for example mobile phone money services, such as IMPS in India, which provides payment services.

2.1.2 Digital Currencies (DCs): Digital currencies (DCs) are digital representations of value, currently issued by private developers and denominated in their own unit of account. They are obtained, stored, accessed, and transacted electronically and neither denominated in any sovereign currency nor issued or backed by any government or central bank.

DCs are not necessarily attached to a fiat currency, but are accepted by natural or legal persons as a means of exchange and can be transferred, stored or traded electronically. DC schemes comprise two key elements: (a) the digital representation of value or *currency* that can be transferred between parties and (b) the way in which value is transferred from a payer to a payee.

Privately issued DCs, such as bitcoin, facilitate peer-to-peer exchange, possibly at lower cost for end-users and with faster transaction times, especially across borders. DC schemes are also known as *crypto currencies* due to their use of cryptographic techniques.

Crypto currencies derive their value solely from the expectation that others will be willing to exchange it for sovereign currency or goods and services. DC schemes may allow for the issuance of a limited or unlimited number of units. In most digital currency schemes, distributed ledger technology allows for remote peer-to-peer exchanges of electronic value. The various DC schemes differ from each other in a number of ways; they have different rules for supplying the currency; they differ in the way in which transactions are verified.

The implications of DCs for financial firms, markets and system will depend on the extent of their acceptability among users. If use of DCs were to become widespread, it would likely have material implications for the business models of financial institutions. DCs could potentially lead to a disintermediation of some existing payment services infrastructure.

Presently, DCs schemes are not widely used or accepted, and they face a series of challenges that could limit their future growth. As a result, their influence on financial services and the wider economy is negligible, and it is possible that in the long-run they may remain a product for a limited user base on the fringes of mainstream financial services.

The regulatory perimeter around DCs is a complicated issue and regulation may depend on the definition of DCs in particular jurisdictions. The cross-border reach of DC schemes may make it difficult for national authorities to enforce laws.

2.1.3 Distributed Ledgers Technology (DLT): DLT provides complete and secure transaction records, updated and verified by users, removing the need for a central authority. These technologies allow for direct peer-to-peer transactions, which might offer benefits, in terms of efficiency and security, over existing technological solutions.

The impetus behind the development and adoption of distributed ledger technology are the potential benefits. The major benefits are as under:

1. Reduced cost.
2. Faster settlement time.
3. Reduction in counterparty risk.
4. Reduced need for third party intermediation.
5. Reduced collateral demand and latency.
6. Better fraud prevention.
7. Greater resiliency.
8. Simplification of reporting, data collection, and systemic risk monitoring.
9. Increased interconnectedness.
10. Privacy.

DLT is an innovation with potentially broad applications in financial market infrastructures (FMIs) and in the economy as a whole. Its most common use at present is for digital currencies, but firms are stepping up their R&D activities for other uses including securities trading, smart contracts, and land and credit registries. If widely adopted, distributed ledger technology can pose new challenges for regulation. Though there are no imminent concerns, constant monitoring of developments in the application of the distributed ledger technology to financial services and systems is prudent given the significant potential of the technology.

2.1.4 Blockchain Technology: Blockchain is a distributed ledger in which transactions—e.g. involving digital currencies or securities—are stored as blocks (groups of transactions that are performed around the same point in time) on computers that are connected to the network. The ledger grows as the chain of blocks increases in size. Each new block of transactions has to be verified by the network before it can be added to the chain. This means that each computer connected to the network has full information about the transactions in the network. Block chain potentially has far-reaching implications for the financial sector, and this is prompting more and more banks, insurers and other financial institutions to invest in research into potential applications of this technology.

Frequently cited benefits of block chain are its transparency, security and the fact that transactions are logged in the network. Some of the disadvantages include the lack of co-ordination and the scalability of this technology. One of the best-known applications of block chain technology at the present time is bitcoin. Transactions in this virtual currency are largely anonymous. This creates ethical risks for financial institutions dealing with users of this currency, because they are unable to fully verify their identity.

It has also been observed that market participants in other securities markets are exploring the usage of block chain or distributed database technology to provide various services such as clearing and settlement, trading etc. Indian securities market may also see such developments in the near future and, therefore, there is a need to understand the benefits, risks and challenges such developments may pose.

2.2 Deposits, Lending and Capital Raising Services

Alternative models of lending and capital raising are gaining prominence, potentially changing the market dynamics of traditional lenders and affecting the role of traditional intermediaries. A few examples of the products offered by FinTechs are as under:

2.2.1 Peer-to-peer (P2P) Lending: P2P lenders connect lenders and borrowers, using advanced technologies to speed up loan acceptance. These technologies are designed to increase the efficiency and reduce the time involved in access to credit. While P2P lending originally involved direct matching of individual lenders and borrowers on a one-to-one basis, it has evolved into a form of market place lending where institutional and high net worth individual investors lend into a pool that borrowers can access.

Depending on the structure, P2P may involve simple matching, deposit taking, or management of a collective investment scheme. Since P2P lending companies operate entirely online, they can run with lower overhead costs and provide services more cheaply than traditional financial institutions. As a result, lenders often earn higher returns compared to savings and investment products offered by banks, while borrowers can borrow money at lower interest rates. The most common form of P2P loan is an unsecured personal loan, but start-up and small-business loans are also becoming important. The principal benefit of P2P lending for borrowers is the fast and convenient access to funding, while for investors it is the potential for high returns.

In their current form, P2P platforms are different from banks, because they do not take positions in loans and do not generally perform maturity and liquidity transformation like banks. P2P platforms more directly match the risk appetite of lenders with the risk profile of borrowers. These factors are likely to make P2P platforms less systemically important than banks of comparable size.

The default of a bank can have systemic effects because of the many credit inter linkages that a bank builds during its business of intermediating credit markets. This creates the possibility of contagion should a single bank fail. The risk of such a contagion is likely to be much less with the failure of a P2P platform because they do not have the same network of credit inter-linkages. This would be true even if a P2P platform was very large. In sum, P2P lending does not currently pose a systemic risk, and it is not clear whether it would if the sector grew significantly larger.

2.2.2 Crowd Funding: Crowd funding is a way of raising debt or equity from multiple investors via an internet-based platform. Securities and Exchange Board of India (SEBI) has defined crowd funding as "solicitation of funds (small amount) from multiple investors through a web-based platform or social networking site for a specific project, business venture or social cause". Some jurisdictions have chosen to enact special legislative regimes to determine the conditions under which this service can be made available to retail investors. The platform matches borrowers/issuers with savers/investors. Platform providers offer a range of information about the potential borrowers/issuers, ranging from credit ratings (for most peer-to-peer loan arrangements) to business model to verification of information of firms that want to raise equity capital.

2.3 Market Provisioning Services

Advances in computing power are facilitating faster and cheaper provision of information and services to the market. A few of these innovations are discussed below:

2.3.1 Smart Contracts: Smart contracts are computer protocols that can self-execute, self-enforce, self-verify, and self-constrain the performance of a contract. Development of smart contracts in relation to financial services could have a large impact on the structure of trade finance or derivatives trading, especially more bespoke contracts, and could also be integrated into Robo-advice wealth management services. The widespread adoption of smart contracts in financial services could be facilitated by the establishment of distributed ledger technology.

2.3.2 E-aggregators: E-aggregators provide internet-based venues for retail customers to compare the prices and features of a range of financial (and non-financial) products such as standardised insurance, mortgages, and deposit account products. They can also be firms that provide services that allow users to aggregate and analyse their data on their payment patterns, across separate accounts and products (e.g. Yodlee). E-aggregators also provide an easy way to switch between providers and may become a major distributor for a variety of financial products.

Reserve Bank of India (RBI) has issued directions regarding account aggregators which require that no entity other than a company can undertake the business of an account aggregator, no company shall commence or carry on the business as an account aggregator without obtaining a certificate of registration from the RBI and every company seeking registration with the RBI as non-banking financial company, account aggregator shall have a net owned fund of not less than ₹ 2 crore or such higher amount, as the RBI may specify. Provided that, entities being regulated by other financial sector regulators and aggregating only those accounts relating to the financial assets of that particular sector will be excluded from the registration requirement.

2.3.3 Cloud Computing: Cloud-based IT services can deliver internet-based access to a shared pool of computing resources that can be quickly and easily deployed. Infrastructure, platform service and mobile back-end as a service are offered under cloud-based services. The use of these services is an important enabler for new entrants to the financial services arena to set up quickly and with low start-up cost; with easy options to expand their capability as the firm grows.

2.3.4 Big Data: As more business activity is digitised, new sources of information are becoming available. Combining these data sources with the availability of increased computing power is delivering faster, cheaper, and more comprehensive analysis for better informed decision-making. For example, wider use of increasingly large datasets could deliver material improvements in credit risk assessments. Financial institutions may desire to monetize aggregated data by selling them or bundling them with other products and services offered.

2.3.5 Artificial Intelligence (AI) and Robotics: Companies looking to achieve a competitive edge through AI need to work through the implications of machines that can learn, conduct human interactions, and engage in other high-level functions at an unmatched scale and speed. They need to identify what machines do better than humans and vice versa, develop complementary roles and responsibilities for each, and redesign processes accordingly. AI often requires a new structure, of both centralized and decentralized activities, that can be challenging to implement. Finally, companies need to embrace the adaptive and agile ways of working and setting strategies that are common at start-ups and AI pioneers.

2.3.6 Robo Advice: Robo advice is the provision of financial advice by automated, money management providers, thereby disintermediating human financial advisors and reducing costs. It can offer more investor choice, especially for low and middle income investors who do not have access to the wealth management divisions of the banks. Robo advisors use client information and algorithms to develop automated portfolio allocation and investment recommendations that are meant to be tailored to the needs of individual clients.

2.3.7 Electronic Trading (E-trading): E-trading has become an increasingly important part of the market landscape, notably in fixed income markets. It has enabled a pickup of automated trading in the most liquid market segments. Innovative trading venues and protocols, reinforced by changes in the nature of intermediation, have proliferated, and new market participants have emerged. This, in turn, has implications for the process of price discovery and for market liquidity. It could also lead market structures to evolve from over-the-counter to a structure where all-to-all transactions can take place. The development of e-trading platforms has contributed to improving the efficiency of market orders and to reducing average trading costs.

3

Artificial Intelligence (AI)

Artificial intelligence has applications in the financial industry, where it is used to detect and flag activity in banking and finance such as unusual debit card usage and large account deposits—all of which help a bank's fraud department. Applications for AI are also being used to help streamline and make trading easier. This is done by making supply, demand, and pricing of securities easier to estimate.

3.1 What is AI?

Artificial intelligence (AI) refers to the simulation of human intelligence in machines that are programmed to think like humans and mimic their actions. The term may also be applied to any machine that exhibits traits associated with a human mind such as learning and problem-solving. The ideal characteristic of artificial intelligence is its ability to rationalize and take actions that have the best chance of achieving a specific goal. A sub-set of artificial intelligence is machine learning, which refers to the concept that computer programmes can automatically learn from and adapt to new data without being assisted by humans. Deep learning techniques enable this automatic learning through the absorption of huge amounts of unstructured data such as text, images, or video.

Artificial intelligence is based on the principle that human intelligence can be defined in a way that a machine can easily mimic it and execute tasks, from the most simple to those that are even more complex. The goals of artificial intelligence include mimicking human cognitive activity. Researchers and developers in the field are making surprisingly rapid strides in mimicking activities such as learning, reasoning, and perception, to the extent that these can be concretely defined. Some believe that innovators may soon be able to develop systems that exceed the capacity of humans to learn or reason out any subject. But others remain sceptical because all cognitive activity is laced with value judgments that are subject to human experience.

As technology advances, previous benchmarks that defined artificial intelligence become outdated. For example, machines that calculate basic functions or recognize text through optical character recognition are no longer considered to embody artificial intelligence, since this function is now taken for granted as an inherent computer function.

AI is continuously evolving to benefit many different industries. Machines are wired using a cross-disciplinary approach based on mathematics, computer science, linguistics, psychology, and more. Algorithms often play a very important part in the structure of artificial intelligence, where simple algorithms are used in simple applications, while more complex ones help frame strong artificial intelligence.

3.1.1 Weak and Strong AI: Artificial intelligence can be divided into two different categories: weak and strong. Weak artificial intelligence embodies a system designed to carry out one particular job. Weak AI systems include video games and personal assistants such as Amazon's Alexa and Apple's Siri. You ask the assistant a question, it answers it for you.

Strong artificial intelligence systems are systems that carry on the tasks considered to be human-like. These tend to be more complex and complicated systems. They are programmed to handle situations in which they may be required to solve problems without having a person intervene. These kinds of systems can be found in applications like self-driving cars or in hospital operating rooms.

3.2 Applications of AI

When most people hear the term artificial intelligence, the first thing they usually think of is robots. That is because big-budget films and novels weave stories about human-like machines that wreak havoc on Earth.

Shakey, a mobile robot, was developed in the late 1960s at the Stanford Research Institute, Menlo Park, California. The robot was equipped with a television camera, a range finder, and collision sensors that enabled a minicomputer to control its actions remotely. Shakey could perform a few basic actions, such as go forward, turn, and push, albeit at a very slow pace. Contrasting colours, particularly the dark baseboard on each wall, helped the robot to distinguish separate surfaces.

The applications for artificial intelligence are endless. The technology can be applied to many different sectors and industries. AI is being tested and used in the healthcare industry for dosing drugs and different treatment in patients, and for surgical procedures in the operating room.

Other examples of machines with artificial intelligence include computers that play chess and self-driving cars. Each of these machines must weigh the consequences of any action they take, as each action will impact the end result. In chess, the end result is winning the game. For self-driving cars, the computer system must account for all external data and compute it to act in a way that prevents a collision.

In cognitive simulation, computers are used to test theories about how the human mind works—for example, theories about how people recognize faces or recall memories. Cognitive simulation is already a powerful tool in both neuroscience and cognitive psychology.

3.3 Components of AI

Research in AI has focused chiefly on the following components of intelligence: learning, reasoning, problem solving, perception, and using language.

3.3.1 Learning: There are a number of different forms of learning as applied to artificial intelligence. The simplest is learning by trial and error as, for example, a simple computer programme for solving mate-in-one chess problems might try moves at random until mate is found. The program might then store the solution with the position so that the next time the computer encountered the same position it would recall the solution. This simple memorizing of individual items and procedures—known as rote learning—is relatively easy to implement on a computer. More challenging is the problem of implementing what is called generalization. Generalization involves applying past experience to analogous new situations. For example, a program that learns the past tense of regular English verbs by rote will not be able to produce the past tense of a word such as *jump* unless it previously had been presented with *jumped*, whereas a program that is able to generalize can learn the "add *ed*" rule and so form the past tense of *jump* based on experience with similar verbs.

3.3.2 Reasoning: To reason is to draw inferences appropriate to the situation Inferences are classified as either deductive or inductive. An example of deductive reasoning is, "Ankit must be either at home or in the office. He is not at home. Therefore he is in the office". Example of inductive reasoning can be, "Previous accidents of this sort were caused by break failure. Therefore, this accident was caused by break failure". The most significant difference between these forms of reasoning is that in the deductive case the truth of the premises guarantees the truth of the conclusion, whereas in the inductive case the truth of the premise lends support to the conclusion without giving absolute assurance. Inductive reasoning is common in science, where data are collected and tentative models are developed to describe and predict future behaviour—until the appearance of anomalous data forces the model to be revised. Deductive reasoning is common in mathematics and logic, where elaborate structures of irrefutable theorems are built up from a small set of basic axioms and rules.

There has been considerable success in programming computers to draw inferences, especially deductive inferences. However, true reasoning involves more than just drawing inferences. It involves drawing inferences *relevant* to the solution of the particular task or situation. This is one of the hardest problems confronting AI.

3.3.3 Problem Solving: Problem solving, particularly in artificial intelligence, may be characterized as a systematic search through a range of possible actions in order to reach some predefined goal or solution. Problem-solving methods divide into special purpose and general purpose. A special-purpose method is tailor-made for a particular problem and often exploits very specific features of the situation in which the problem is embedded. In contrast, a general-purpose method is applicable to a wide variety of problems. One general-purpose technique used in AI is means-end analysis—a step-by-step, or incremental, reduction of the difference between the current state and the final goal. The programme selects actions from a list of means—in the case of a simple robot this might consist of pick up, put down, move forward, move back, move left, and move right—until the goal is reached.

Many diverse problems have been solved by artificial intelligence programs. Some examples are finding the winning move (or sequence of moves) in a board game, devising mathematical proofs, and manipulating "virtual objects" in a computer-generated world.

3.3.4 Perception: In perception the environment is scanned by means of various sensory organs, real or artificial, and the scene is decomposed into separate objects in various spatial relationships. Analysis is complicated by the fact that an object may appear different depending on the angle from which it is viewed, the direction and intensity of illumination in the scene, and how much the object contrasts with the surrounding field.

At present, artificial perception is sufficiently well-advanced to enable optical sensors to identify individuals, autonomous vehicles to drive at moderate speeds on the open road, and robots to roam through buildings collecting empty plastic water bottles.

3.3.5 Language: A language is a system of signs having meaning by convention. In this sense, language need not be confined to the spoken word. Traffic signs, for example, form a mini-language, it being a matter of convention that ⚠ means *hazard ahead* in some countries. It is distinctive of languages that linguistic units possess meaning by convention, and linguistic meaning is very different from what is called natural meaning, exemplified in statements such as "Those clouds mean rain" and "The fall in pressure means the valve is malfunctioning".

An important characteristic of full-fledged human languages—in contrast to birdcalls and traffic signs—is their productivity. A productive language can formulate an unlimited variety of sentences.

3.4 Methods and Objectives of AI

AI research follows two distinct, and to some extent competing, methods, viz. the connectionist (or bottom-up) approach and symbolic (or top-down) approach, The bottom-up approach involves creating artificial neural networks in imitation of the brain's structure—hence the *connectionist* label. The top-down approach, on the other and, seeks to replicate intelligence by analyzing cognition independent of the biological structure of the brain, in terms of the processing of symbols—hence the *symbolic* label.

To illustrate the difference between these approaches, consider the task of building a system, equipped with an optical scanner, that recognizes the letters of the alphabet. A bottom-up approach typically involves training an artificial neural network by presenting letters to it one by one, gradually improving performance by *tuning* the network. Tuning adjusts the responsiveness of different neural pathways to different stimuli. In contrast, a top-down approach typically involves writing a computer programme that compares each letter with geometric descriptions. Simply put, neural activities are the basis of the bottom-up approach, while symbolic descriptions are the basis of the top-down approach.

The ultimate ambition of strong AI is to produce a machine whose overall intellectual ability is indistinguishable from that of a human being. This goal generated great interest in the 1950s and 1960s, but such optimism has given way to an appreciation of the extreme difficulties involved. To date, progress has been meagre. Some critics doubt whether research will produce even a system with the overall intellectual ability of a rat in the foreseeable future. Indeed, some researchers view strong AI as not worth pursuing.

Applied AI, also known as advanced information processing, aims to produce commercially viable *smart* systems—for example, expert medical diagnosis systems and stock-trading systems. Applied AI has enjoyed considerable success.

3.5 Is Strong AI Possible?

The ongoing success of applied AI and of cognitive simulation seems assured. However, strong AI, i.e. artificial intelligence that aims to duplicate human intellectual abilities remains controversial Exaggerated claims of success, in professional journals as well as the popular press, have damaged its reputation. At the present time even an embodied system displaying the overall intelligence of a cockroach is proving elusive, let alone a system that can rival a human being.

The difficulty of scaling up AI's modest achievements cannot be overstated. Five decades of research in symbolic AI have failed to produce any firm evidence that a symbol system can manifest human levels of general intelligence.

Connectionists are unable to model the nervous systems of even the simplest invertebrates. Critics of AI regard as simply mystical the view that high-level behaviours involving language understanding, planning, and reasoning will somehow emerge from the interaction of basic behaviours such as obstacle avoidance, gaze control, and object manipulation.

In fact, AI has no real definition of intelligence to offer, not even in the sub-human case. Rats are intelligent, but what exactly must an artificial intelligence achieve before researchers can claim this level of success? In the absence of a reasonably precise criterion for when an artificial system counts as intelligent, there is no objective way of telling whether an AI research programme has succeeded or failed.

3.6 Issues and Concerns

Since its beginning, artificial intelligence has come under scrutiny from scientists and the public alike. One common theme is the idea that machines will become so highly developed that humans will not be able to keep up and they will take off on their own, redesigning themselves at an exponential rate.

Another is that machines can hack into people's privacy and even be weaponized. Other arguments debate the ethics of artificial intelligence and whether intelligent systems such as robots should be treated with the same rights as humans.

Self-driving cars have been fairly controversial as their machines tend to be designed for the lowest possible risk and the least casualties. If presented with a scenario of colliding with one person or another at the same time, these cars would calculate the option that would cause the least amount of damage.

Another contentious issue many people have with artificial intelligence is how it may affect human employment. With many industries looking to automate certain jobs through the use of intelligent machinery, there is a concern that people would be pushed out of the workforce. Self-driving cars may remove the need for taxis and car-share programmes, while manufacturers may easily replace human labour with machines, making people's skills more obsolete.

To sum up, the term artificial intelligence is frequently applied to developing systems endowed with intellectual processes characteristic of humans, such as the ability to reason, discover meaning, generalize, or learn from past experience. Since the development of the digital computer in the 1940s, it has been demonstrated that computers can be programmed to carry out very complex tasks—as, for example, discovering proofs for mathematical theorems or playing chess—with great proficiency.

Still, despite continuing advances in computer processing speed and memory capacity, there are as yet no programmes that can match human flexibility over wider domains or in tasks requiring much everyday knowledge. On the other hand, some programmes have attained the performance levels of human experts and professionals in performing certain specific tasks, so that artificial intelligence in this limited sense is found in applications as diverse as medical diagnosis, computer search engines, and voice or handwriting recognition.

Part II
Digital Banking in India

4

Digital Banking and India's Digital Competitiveness

4.1 Significance of Digitization

Digitization is the process by which technology lowers the costs of storing, sharing, and analyzing data. This process has changed how financial institutions behave, how industrial activities are organized, and how governments operate.

Digitization has coincided with the increased prominence of platforms and marketplaces that connect diverse agents in social and economic activity. Platforms are most readily identified with their technical standards, i.e. engineering specifications for hardware and standards for software. The pricing and product strategies that platforms use differ from those of traditional firms because of the presence of network effects. Network effects are within platforms because participation by one group affects the utility of another group. Furthermore, network effects make the analysis of competition between platforms more complex than the analysis of competition between traditional firms.

Digitization has partially or fully replaced many tasks that were previously done by human labourers. At the same time, computers have made some workers much more productive. Another consequence of digitization is that it has drastically reduced the costs of communication between workers across different organizations and locations. This has led to a change in the geographic and contractual organization of production.

4.1.1 Digital Economy: It refers to an economy that is based on digital technologies. The digital economy is also sometimes called the *internet economy*, *new economy*, or *web economy*. Increasingly, the *digital economy* is intertwined with the traditional economy making a clear delineation harder.

In this new economy, digital networking and communication infrastructures provide a global platform over which people and organizations devise strategies, interact, communicate, collaborate and search for information.

It is widely accepted that the growth of the digital economy has widespread impact on the whole economy. Various attempts at categorising the size of the impact on traditional sectors have been made.

Given its expected broad impact, traditional firms are actively assessing how to respond to the changes brought about by the digital economy. For corporations, timing of their response is of the essence. Banks are trying to innovate and use digital tools to improve their traditional business.

4.2 Digitization in Banking Sector

Information technology (IT) has transformed the functioning of businesses, the world over. It has: (a) bridged the gaps in terms of the reach and the coverage of systems (b) enabled better decision-making based on latest and accurate information, (c) reduced costs and (d) improved overall improvement in efficiency. In the Indian context, the financial sector, especially the banking sector, has been a major beneficiary from the inroads made by IT. Many new processes, products and services offered by banks and other financial intermediaries are now IT-centred.

Banks have traditionally been in the forefront of harnessing technology to improve their products, services and efficiency. They have, over a long time, been using electronic and telecommunication networks for delivering a wide range of value-added products and services. The delivery channels include, inter alia, direct dial-up connections, private networks, public networks and the devices including telephone, personal computers (PCs), automated teller machines (ATMs), networking of ATMs in the form of shared payment networks, and core banking solutions.

With the popularity of PCs, easy access to internet and

world wide web (www), internet is increasingly used by banks as a channel for receiving instructions and delivering their products and services to their customers. This form of banking is generally referred to as internet banking, although the range of products and services offered by different banks vary widely both in their content and sophistication. Effective integration of technology with sound business practices requires business process re-engineering and banks in India need to follow up on the beginnings made in this regard.

Reserve Bank of India (RBI) has played a proactive role in the implementation of IT in the banking sector. IT-based initiatives are focused on meeting the three-pronged objective of better house keeping, improved customer service and overall systemic efficiency.

India with its uniquely rich payment ecosystem is now emerging as a global leader in innovative population scale payment systems. RBI and the Government have articulated a vision of a less-cash society and guided its evolution with feet firmly on the ground.

The growth of financial services in India has largely been led by the banks. RBI and the banks have led the initial thrust, development and support of digital payments infrastructure and systems. Non-banks have entered the market and expanded the range of payment services available to the Indian clients backed by their strength in technology and customer-centric innovation. Banks and non-banks are partnering to offer the combination of trust and innovations to the Indian customers.

4.2.1 Responsibility of Banks in the Emerging Scenario: The country is going through a significant change, in the digitization of the economy, and the payments system. As a result, there will be many individuals who are new to digitization, formalization, and payment systems. They will require help, and they will look to the banking systems to provide that help (in so far as digital banking and payments are concerned). However, such a capacity is also seen to be missing within the banking system.

Digital payments are growing rapidly and are seeing adoption across the country. While the technology continues to evolve, newer users are continuously engaging with the payment system. It is important that these users are educated about the benefits and dangers of digital payments. They must also be made aware of their rights, and the importance of protecting their data and privacy. In addition, the users must be educated on how they can get redress for any problems that they face while accessing the system.

So, while the banks are working towards educating the customers, they must also look to build capacity within the banking system, bank employees, agents, etc., so that they in turn can help educate the customers and take the country along in this transformation. All branch staff, call centre staff and frontline agents must be aware of the bank's digital products and be able to educate customers. They can then help create digital habits with the customer. Additional capacity is required in the financial service providers, and in the technology service providers to ensure that the newer payment systems continue to operate and scale smoothly, and are protected from security threats, etc.

4.3 What is Digital Payment?

India has a rich diversity of digital payment options. Many of these are interoperable, and work through bank accounts, thus giving the users a lot more choice. However, the costs of digital payments are still an issue, and acceptance infrastructure is not widespread.

According to RBI's Ombudsman Scheme for digital transactions, "*digital transaction* means a payment transaction in a seamless system effected without the need for cash at least in one of the two legs, if not in both. This includes transactions made through digital/electronic modes wherein both the originator and the beneficiary use digital/electronic medium to send or receive money". [1]

4.4 Benefits of Digital Payments

These are as under:

4.4.1 Common Man:

1. Reduced cash and hence more safety.
2. Faster payment.
3. Reduced number of visits to bank.
4. Interest earning on money in the bank.

4.4.2 Vendors:

1. Transactions settled quickly.
2. Getting rid of coins and change.
3. Larger transactions made easy.
4. Improved accounting and book keeping.
5. No need to keep large amounts of cash.

4.5 Role of RBI in Promoting Digital Payments

Digital payments are an important means of economic development and achieving financial inclusion. The task of deepening digital payments is onerous but not insurmountable. It requires concerted effort of all the stake holders to work together with the aim of achieving a digitally included society.

Reserve Bank of India (RBI) has been taking many initiatives for encouraging digitisation of payments in the country. Significant inroads have been made in making available a variety of digital payment options and with time their usage has increased. RBI also publishes, from time-to-time, its Vision Document for Payment and Settlement Systems in India, the last being released in May 2019 for the period 2019-21.

In recent years, Government of India and RBI have set up various committees for understanding the needs of the payments eco-system and suggesting suitable measures for enhancing the penetration and usage of digital payments. Some of these committees were as under:

1. Committee on Medium-term Path for Financial Inclusion (Chairman: Deepak Mohanty).
2. Committee of Chief Ministers on Digital Payments

(Chairman: Chandra Babu Naidu).

3. Committee to Review the Framework Related to Digital Payments (Chairman: R.P. Watal).
4. Steering Committee on Fintech Related Issues (Chairman: S.C. Garg).
5. Inter-regulatory Working Group on Fintech and Digital Banking (Chairman: Sudarshan Sen).
6. High-Level Committee on Deepening of Digital Payments (Chairman: Nandan Nilekani), May 2019.

Above committees made important recommendations which had significant impact on the present payment systems.

4.6 Data on Payment Systems

RBI collects, and publishes data related on payment systems in a monthly bulletin. This includes data on large value payment systems such as real time gross settlement system (RTGS) and also retail payment systems covering paper [cheque truncation system (CTS), express cheque clearing system (ECCS)], retail electronic payment systems [national electronic funds transfer (NEFT), immediate payment service (IMPS), National Automated Clearing House (NACH), electronic clearing service (ECS)] and card payments [credit card and debit card usage at POS and online and pre-paid payment instruments (PPIs) in the form of wallets and cards]. RBI also collects data on unified payments interface (BHIM UPI), and other payments (such as AEPS), which are not included in this bulletin.

Post-demonetization, the Ministry of Electronics and Information Technology (MeitY) was made the nodal agency for the *Digi Dhan* mission, and has commenced publication of transaction volume data through the Digidhan Dashboard. The data elements included are RTGS, NEFT, NACH, IMPS, BHIM UPI, BHIM Aadhaar, NETC, AEPS, credit cards, debit cards, PPIs, mobile banking, internet banking, closed system PPIs and others.

Although MeitY sources data from RBI and NPCI among

others, it is observed that the data coverage of RBI and MeitY is different. This could be attributed to the fact that MeitY measures the digital transactions undertaken while RBI focuses on the transactions pertaining to Payment System (regulated by the RBI under the PSS Act). Some of the transactions monitored by MeitY are by entities that are not regulated by the RBI as payment systems. Additionally, some other transactions are considered by the RBI to be banking transactions, and not payment transactions.

In order to ensure consistency, and accuracy of data disseminated to the public, it is essential that all data should be available through a single source. This data must be a by-product of the transaction and not be forced for the purpose of measurements.

Hence, High-Level Committee on Deepening of Digital Payments (Chairman: Nandan Nilekani) recommended that, "RBI should be the single source of accurate and complete information for digital payments data for India. RBI may rationalize digital payments definition for better tracking and include all information that can be captured accurately. It may include unregulated sources where possible. RBI should start publishing data on mobile banking and internet banking along with the split of inter-bank and intra-bank transactions, as these services are provided by banks to facilitate payments". [2]

4.7 Cashless Transactions: India versus Other Countries

Magnitude of cashless transactions in a country can be measured by the number of cashless transactions per capita per annum. Trends in cashless transactions per capita per year in India in recent years are shown in Table 4.1. Annual cashless transactions per capita for select countries are shown in Table 4.2.

4.8 World Digital Competitiveness Ranking, 2019 and India

World Digital Competitiveness Ranking is prepared by IMD (International Institute for Management Development) World Competitiveness Centre based in Lausanne (Switzerland). The ranking has relevance to answer the following questions:

Table 4.1: Trends in Cashless Transactions Per Capita Per Year in India in Recent Years

Year	Number of cashless transactions
2014	2.38
2015	4.06
2016	5.44
2017	10.73
2018	13.15
2019	22.42
2021 (estimated)	220.00

Source: Reserve Bank of India, *Report of the High-Level Committee on Deepening of Digital Payments* (Chairman: Nandan Nilekani), May 2019, p. 23.

Table 4.2: Annual Cashless Transactions Per Capita in Select Countries

S. No.	Country	Number of cashless transactions per capita in 2017
1.	Singapore	782.4
2.	Sweden	497.9
3.	USA	473.6
4.	Euro Area	186.8
5.	Russia	178.5
6.	Brazil	148.5
7.	China	96.7
8.	South Africa	79.2
9.	Indonesia	34.0
10.	**India**	**10.73**

Source: Reserve Bank of India, *Report of the High-Level Committee on Deepening of Digital Payments* (Chairman: Nandan Nilekani), May 2019, pp. 22-23.

1. How prepared are economies to productively use the transformative technologies of our time?

2. Do countries have a feasible framework to facilitate the adoption and use of digitalization?
3. And how ready are they to embrace the implications of digital disruption?

Started in 2017, the ranking measures the capacity and readiness of 63 economies to develop, adopt and explore digital technologies as a key driver for economic transformation in business, government and wider society.

The index ranks the countries based on the following three factors:

1. **Knowledge:** The capacity to understand and learn new technologies.
2. **Technology:** The competence to develop new digital innovations.
3. **Future Readiness:** The preparedness for the coming developments.

The first factor, knowledge, refers to the intangible infrastructure, which underlines the process of digital transformation through the discovery, understanding and learning of new technologies.

The technology factor assesses the overall context through which the development of digital technologies is enabled. Technology not only affects how businesses perform but also how economies function and prepare for the future. Governments around the world are investing heavily in their digital economy to enhance value creation and prosperity.

Finally, the future readiness factor is one that examines the level of preparedness of an economy to assume its digital transformation.

In the 2021 Digital Competitiveness Index, USA ranked as the most digitally competitive country in the world, followed by Hong Kong, Sweden, Denmark and Singapore. India ranked at the 44th place (Table 4.3) It ranked at 48th position in 2018. Its position improved overall in all factors including knowledge, technology and future readiness in exploring more digital technologies.

Table 4.3: Digital Competitive Ranking, 2021
Top Ten plus China and India

Country	Rank	Score (0-100)
USA	1	100.00
Hong Kong	2	96.58
Sweden	3	95.19
Denmark	4	95.16
Singapore	5	95.14
Switzerland	6	94.94
Netherlands	7	93.31
Taiwan	8	92.24
Norway	9	91.30
UAE	10	90.52
China	**15**	**84.43**
India	**44**	**55.13**

Source: IMD World Competitiveness Centre, *World Digital Competitiveness Ranking, 2021*.

The results of the 2021 ranking showed that top performing countries largely focused on the factors that contribute to the generation of knowledge. Western economies remain as the main digital hubs and leaders as global knowledge centres. Several Asian economies improved this year reducing the digital gap mainly through advancement in the technology and future readiness factors.

However, it seems that they remain dependent of western economies for the generation of knowledge. In addition, the data show that factors related to political stability affect the availability of funding technological development. This is particularly relevant for SMEs in countries with limited political stability.

4.9 Digital Payments Index of RBI

It captures the extent of digitization of payments across the country. The index captures the following:

1. Payment enablers (weight 25 percent).
2. Payment infrastructure–Demand side factors (10 percent).

3. Payment Infrastructure–Supply side factors (15 percent).
4. Payment performance (45 percent).
5. Consumer centricity (5 percent).

Digital Payments Index increased from 100 in March 2018 (base period) to 304.06 in September 2021.

Endnotes

1. RBI Ombudsman Scheme for Digital Payments. https://rbidocs.rbi.org.in/rdocs/Content/PDFs/OSDT31012019.pdf.
2. Reserve Bank of India, *Report of the High-Level Committee on Deepening of Digital Payments* (Chairman: Nandan Nilekani), May 2019, p. 21.

5

Importance and Forms of Payment Systems

Under a system of simple commodity production, exchange of goods was accomplished largely through barter. The main difficulty of the barter system was the double coincidence of wants. In a modern economy, characterised by acute specialisation and exchange, barter system would just be impossible. It is, therefore, necessary to accept some one thing as a medium of exchange. Any generally accepted thing which serves as a medium of exchange may be called money. Historically, a variety of things have served as money including goats, coins, paper currency and demand deposits of banks.

The first and the most important function of money is to act as a medium of exchange. As a matter of fact, money is defined in terms of this unique function. Other functions of money are more or less derived from this function. By using money as a medium of exchange, a society can get rid of the difficulties of the barter system. By the use of money, exchange becomes easy and this promotes specialisation which has its own advantages in a modern society.

5.1 Money and Payment Obligations

Use of money for settlement of payment obligations has a very long history. Use of non-cash exchange through barter preceded the introduction of money. Barter, however, co-exists with monetised economy in some underdeveloped agricultural societies even now. But currency or cash is the most readily accepted medium of exchange in all modern societies because it is the legal tender and helps to bring about irrevocable settlement.

There are, however, certain disadvantages associated with the use of cash. Holding cash does not fetch any return-the interest foregone because of cash holding is a cost to the holder of cash. Besides, the holder of cash bears some insurance costs in terms of the premiums that are paid to cover any loss/theft. Moreover, carrying of large quantities of cash to make large-value payments is a security risk and also involves transportation costs.

Payment and settlement systems form the backbone of any economy. The spectacular growth in financial transactions has necessitated certain radical changes in the payments and settlement systems around the globe. The technological revolution in the field of electronics and telecommunications has helped to bring about sophisticated developments in the payments and settlement systems in many countries. A well defined payments and settlement system is, therefore, a crucial component of the financial infrastructure of any country.

Payments system provides the arteries or highways for conducting trade, commerce and other forms of economic activities in any country. An efficient payments system functions as a lubricant speeding up the liquidity flow in the economy and creating a momentum for economic growth. The payments process is a vital aspect of financial intermediation; it enables the creation and transfer of liquidity among different economic agents. A smooth, well-functioning payments system not only ensures efficient utilisation of scarce resources but also eliminates systemic risks.

Payments system assumes importance in the context of domestic financial sector reforms and global financial integration. The time value of money flows has increased sharply in view of the competing demands on the financial sector. Efficient, low cost cross-border payments flow helps to promote international trade in goods and services. Foreign investments (direct and portfolio) are encouraged by the availability of an efficient payments system. For these reasons, an efficient and technologically advanced payments and settlement system performs a vital infrastructural function in the economy. Reserve Bank of India (RBI) has, therefore, been taking measures to set up such an infrastructural set up.

5.2 Importance of a Sound Payment System

The payment and settlement systems are at the core of financial infrastructure in a country. A well-functioning payment and settlement system is crucial for the successful implementation of monetary policy and maintaining the financial stability. Central banks have, therefore, always maintained a keen interest in the development of payment and settlement system as part of their responsibilities for monetary and financial stability. In India, the development of a safe, secure and sound payment and settlement system has been the key policy objective. In this direction, the RBI, apart from performing the regulatory and supervisory functions, has also been making efforts to promote functionality and modernisation of the payment and settlement systems on an ongoing basis.

A safe and efficient payment system is a prerequisite for smooth functioning of the financial markets. The conduct of monetary policy in an effective manner requires safe and efficient payment and settlement systems to facilitate transfer of funds and securities between the central bank and other participants in the financial system. An efficient and stable payment and settlement system is also a pre-condition for inter-bank money markets and other short-term credit markets through which monetary policy is transmitted. In addition, developments in the payment and settlement systems that affect the speed and realisation and availability of funds for further deployment can influence the overall demand for money in the economy.

By linking financial institutions together for the purpose of transferring monetary claims and settling payment obligations, payment and settlement system becomes a channel through which financial risks are transmitted across financial institutions and markets. Well-designed and efficiently managed systems, therefore, help in maintaining financial stability by reducing uncertainty of settlement. Settlement failures which spread to other payment and settlement systems through the contagion effect not only undermine the smooth functioning of the financial markets, but can also adversely affect the public confidence in money and efficacy of the instruments used to transfer money.

Payment and settlement systems, which constitute the backbone of the financial economy, aim at minimising the systemic risk. The payment system influences the speed, financial risk, reliability and the cost of domestic and international transactions. With the significant improvements in payment and settlement systems, depth and liquidity of various segments of the financial market can be improved.

Settlement systems in India have evolved over a period of time from physical settlement systems with considerable amount of risks to the current electronic systems with central counterparty with emphasis on risk mitigation. During the early 1990s, government securities market was opaque with limited information dissemination and inefficient pricing. The securities were held in physical form requiring execution of physical transfer forms for transfer of securities in any trade leading to inefficiencies in settling the trades. Settlement of securities and funds legs were independent of each other (non-DvP), leading to considerable settlement risks. Moreover, pre-settlement comparison and confirmation of trades was not systematised. Settlement cycles were not uniform with settlements happening on T+0 and T+1 basis.

5.3 Forms of Payments

The requirements of a modern economy in regard to settlement of transactions are diverse and variegated and the needs of manufacturing, trade, and commerce activities involve large value payments over vast geographic distances. External trade with the rest of the world involves payments in different currencies. Payments can no longer be completed by simple cash transfer in such cases. Therefore, there arises the need for additional forms of payments, which can be facilitated with improved financial intermediation and expansion of financial instruments. Cheques and other paper-based instruments and to some extent electronic instruments have become important modes of payment in recent times in most countries because of growing financial intermediation.

Individuals, business entities or governments issue cheques or other forms of order on their banks in discharge of their payment obligations. The recipients of these orders would then get the funds embodied in these payment instruments through their own banks. As the number of banks grew over time, the volume of instruments exchanged among them increased substantially. Consequently, as also to have an orderly means of transfer of payment instructions among banks at a location or centre, a common set of practices and mechanisms of exchange had to be evolved. When instruments presented by customers of banks become payable at outside locations, special collection arrangements are set in motion to collect the funds. If the collecting bank has a branch at the relevant outside location, there would be no problem, but, if the collecting bank does not have a branch at the outside location, it will have to enter into correspondent banking relationship with another bank at the said outside location for the purpose of collecting funds.

The payment instruments which are routed through financial intermediaries involve book entries at various levels to transfer funds from one party to the other. The range of intermediation varies to take care of different situations. This may, for instance, consist of instructions to intermediaries to move goods coinciding with the movement of funds as in the case of a letter of credit. Or, the instruction could be for payment of specified sums of money to the bearer of a payment instrument, as in the case of a bearer cheque. In some cases, the payment instruments are negotiable in the sense that they can be transferred from person to person in lieu of cash. In yet other cases, both the ultimate beneficiary and the destination could be pre-determined. In all these cases, banks play a crucial part in conveying, transmitting and carrying out the instructions embodied in the payment instruments.

While doing so, these intermediaries have to settle among

themselves the monetary claims arising from the execution of payment instructions. Thus, whenever non-cash payment instruments are involved, they are accompanied by a chain of related fund transfers as well as a stream of book entries and messages. Banks in turn need an intermediate agency such as the clearing house where these instruments can be exchanged and where the financial claims on one another can be settled through a settlement bank, which is usually the central bank of the country.

Clearing houses facilitate the exchange of instruments and processing of payment instructions at a central point among the participating banks. Clearing houses—manual and paper based—in many advanced countries have gradually extended their range of activities to include automated and electronic means for settlement of payment transactions. Such an evolution is also seen in emerging economies.

Banks, as crucial intermediaries in the payments stream, provide deposit accounts to non bank agents (i.e. individuals, firms/corporate bodies) which are considered as liquid assets and facilitate payments transactions. Banks provide credit facilities so that such payments can be effected with lower working balances. Moreover, they act as conduit through which domestic and international capital markets provide resources to the commercial sector.

5.4 Pre-Independence Payment Systems

The Paper Currency Act of 1861 conferred upon the Government of India the monopoly of note issue bringing to an end note issues of private and Presidency Banks.

In 1881, the Negotiable Instruments Act (NI Act) was enacted, formalising the usage and characteristics of instruments like the cheque, the bill of exchange and promissory note. The NI Act provided a legal framework for non-cash paper payment instruments in India.

With the steady growth in volumes of trade and commerce and the growing confidence of the public in the usage of cheques etc., transactions through the use of these payment instruments grew at a rapid pace. With the development of the banking system and higher turnover in the volume of cheques, the need for an organised cheque clearing process emerged amongst the banks. Clearing associations were formed by the banks in the Presidency towns and the final settlement between member banks was effected by means of cheques drawn upon the Presidency Banks. With the setting up of the Imperial Bank in 1921, settlement was done through cheques drawn on that bank.

The Calcutta Clearing Banks' Association, which was the largest bankers' association at that time, adopted clearing house rules in 1938. The association had twenty-five large banks as its members and eight sub-members. There were two ordinary clearings on each business day, except on Saturday when there was one clearing. However, the association did not cover many banks functioning in Calcutta. The cheques, drafts etc. of such non-clearing banks were collected by the clearing banks only on payment of charges. This affected their business prospects adversely, as the public was not likely to maintain accounts with banks whose cheques suffered a serious handicap of market acceptability.

To overcome this problem, these banks formed themselves into a group called the Metropolitan Banking Association with fifty members, which conducted the Metropolitan Clearing House, in 1939. This association arrived at an understanding with the Calcutta Clearing House in 1940. In addition, two other clearings were conducted in Calcutta: Pioneer Clearing and the Walks Clearing.

The Bombay Clearing House was the only association to conduct clearings in Bombay. It had no parallel systems and institutions comparable to the Metropolitan Clearing House of Calcutta. The uniform procedures and charges for collection of non-clearing banks' cheques, drafts, dividend warrants etc. were adopted by the Bombay Clearing House in 1941-42.

After the setting up of Reserve Bank of India (RBI) under the RBI Act 1935, the clearing houses in the Presidency towns were taken over by the RBI.

5.5 India's Present Payment System Architecture

Payment system architecture in India is based on international benchmarks, and guiding principles. The Payment and Settlement System Act, 2007, provides a comprehensive legal framework for payment and settlement services in India for subjects like authorisation of payment system operators, netting and finality of payment and settlement. The payment system objectives of having a safe, sound, cost-effective and wide distribution network are being met in so far as the large value and countrywide payment and settlement systems are concerned. The grand vision is that cash dominant economy may transit to a predominantly non-cash dominant economy with non-cash transactions primarily in electronic mode, which is the international norm. The existing payment system is being constantly reviewed to suggest an action plan for orderly growth of the payment systems.

Since 2015-16, all segments of electronic payments, particularly retail electronic payments, have shown healthy growth both in terms of volume and value of usage. Real time gross settlement (RTGS) and national electronic funds transfer (NEFT) have particularly registered an impressive growth.

Similarly, with increasing number of banks offering mobile banking services and driven by the growth in e-commerce and use of mobile payment applications, the volume of mobile banking transactions has also witnessed a phenomenal growth.

Card transactions have also grown significantly at both ATMs as well as at the point-of-sale (PoS) with the growth in debit card usage at PoS picking up significantly. The growth in volume and value of transactions using pre-paid payment instruments (PPIs) issued by banks and authorised non-bank entities has also been significant.

The volume and value in immediate payment service (IMPS) has also grown significantly with the development of the IMPS as a multi-channel system providing various options to customers to originate transactions.

Payment systems in India comprise paper-based traditional systems and electronic payment systems. Another classification pertains to large value payment systems and retail payment systems.

6

Reserve Bank of India (RBI) and Payment Systems

Central banks worldwide are involved in payment and settlement systems in a number of ways. They provide settlement accounts, oversee core payment arrangements, and operate, provide and use various payment services.

The central bank of any country is usually the driving force in the development of national payment systems. RBI as the central bank of India has been playing this developmental role and has taken several initiatives for safe, secure, sound, efficient, accessible and authorised payment systems in the country. The RBI has taken many initiatives towards introducing and upgrading safe and efficient modes of payment systems in the country to meet the requirements of the public at large.

Payment and settlement systems are at the heart of a modern economy. Recognising this, RBI has been, over the years, initiating measures that have resulted in the payment systems in India gaining international recognition. The recent past has witnessed significant developments in this area, which have brought in a sea-change in the way our citizens use technology-based systems and products to take care of their funds transfer requirements.

RBI's vision for the payment and settlement systems is to encourage greater use of electronic payments by all sections of society. This is aided by the establishment of a robust backbone to meet the economy's requirements, while ensuring safety, security and universal reach with technological solutions that hasten processing, as also improve the user-convenience dimension. While the RBI continues to pay focused attention to appropriate enabling regulation, strong infrastructure, apposite supervision and customer centricity, due attention must be paid by operators towards cyber security, effective customer grievance redress arrangements and reasonableness of customer charges. Operators should ensure that no corner is cut regarding cyber security.

In India, RBI regulates and supervises payment and settlement systems with the objective of promoting safety and efficiency by monitoring the existing and planned systems, assessing them against the stated objectives and, where necessary, inducing change. The oversight of payment and settlement systems has become more distinct and formal in recent years as part of a growing concern with financial stability as also with the increasing role of private participants in financial transactions. The increasing attention by the RBI also reflects the large increase in the value of transfers cleared and settled, the increasing centralisation of transactions around a small number of key systems and the growing technological complexity.

The initiatives taken by the RBI in the mid-1980s and early-1990s focused on technology-based solutions for the improvement of the payment and settlement system infrastructure, coupled with the introduction of new payment products by taking advantage of the technological advancements in banks. The continued increase in the volume of cheques added pressure on the existing set-up, thus necessitating a cost-effective alternative system.

6.1 Payment and Settlement Systems (PSS) Act, 2007

In India, the payment and settlement systems are regulated by PSS Act, 2007 which was legislated in December 2007. The Act as well as the Payment and Settlement System Regulations, 2008 framed thereunder came into effect from August 12, 2008. PSS Act, 2007 provides for the regulation and supervision of payment systems in India and designates the Reserve Bank of India (RBI) as the authority for that purpose and all related matters. It designates RBI as the authority to regulate payment and settlement systems. Under this Act, RBI has been given wide regulatory and supervisory powers in respect of payment systems. The Act provides for: (a) authorisation by RBI to commence or operate payment systems, (b) empowering the RBI to audit and inspect by entering the premises where payment systems are being operated, (c) empowering RBI to issue directions and (d) finality of settlements (including netting) and their irrevocability in the event of insolvency, overriding other laws.

RBI is authorized under the Act to constitute a Committee of its Central Board known as the Board for Regulation and Supervision of Payment and Settlement Systems (BPSS), to exercise its powers and perform its functions and discharge its duties under this statute. It is the highest policy making body on payment systems in the country. The BPSS is empowered for authorising, prescribing policies and setting standards for regulating and supervising all the payment and settlement systems in the country. The Department of Payment and Settlement Systems of RBI serves as the Secretariat to the Board and executes its directions.

In terms of Section 4 of the PSS Act, no person other than the RBI can commence or operate a payment system in India unless authorised by the RBI. The RBI has since authorised payment system operators of pre-paid payment instruments, card schemes, cross-border in-bound money transfers, ATM networks and centralised clearing arrangements.

The dominant features of large geographic spread of the country and the vast network of branches of the Indian banking system require the logistics of collection and delivery of paper instruments. These aspects of the banking structure in the country have always been kept in mind while developing the payment systems.

At present, payments can be made through paper-based instruments and various types of electronic instruments.

Oversight of the payment and settlement systems is a central bank function whereby the objectives of safety and efficiency are promoted by monitoring existing and planned systems, assessing them against these objectives and, where necessary, inducing change. By overseeing payment and settlement systems, central banks help to maintain systemic stability and reduce systemic risk, and to maintain public confidence in payment and settlement systems.

The Payment and Settlement Systems Act, 2007, and the Payment and Settlement Systems Regulations, 2008, framed there under, provide the necessary statutory backing to the RBI for undertaking the oversight function over the payment and settlement systems in the country.

6.2 Board for Regulation and Supervision of Payment and Settlement Systems (BPSS)

In order to provide focused attention to the payment and settlement systems, the RBI constituted the BPSS as a Committee of its Central Board. The Reserve Bank of India (Board for Regulation and Supervision of Payment and Settlement Systems) Regulations, 2005 was notified in the Gazette of India on February 18, 2005. The BPSS is headed by the Governor of the RBI with the Deputy Governor in-charge of payment and settlement systems as the Vice-Chairman and the other Deputy Governors and two members of the Central Board of the RBI as members. Functions and powers of the BPSS include the following.

1. Formulating policies relating to the regulation and supervision of all types of payment and settlement systems.
2. Setting standards for existing and future systems.
3. Authorising the payment and settlement systems.
4. Determining criteria for membership.

The National Payments Council, which was set up in 1999, has been designated as a Technical Advisory Committee of the BPSS. To assist the BPSS in performing its functions, a new department, the Department of Payments and Settlement Systems (DPSS), was set up in the RBI in March 2005.

The Board at its meetings had emphasised, *inter alia*, the following.

1. Payment system services in India should be taken to a

level comparable with the best in the world.

2. Appropriate legal infrastructure may be created as early as possible.
3. A plan be drawn up to "leapfrog" from cash to electronic modes of payment, wherever possible.
4. Cheque clearing system would have to be made more efficient through cheque truncation system.
5. Usage of the RTGS system be increased both in terms of opening additional branch outlets and more number of transactions being put through.

RBI has taken a number of initiatives to strengthen the institutional, technological and procedural framework for the payment and settlement systems. To carry forward these initiatives in an integrated and cohesive manner, vision documents were prepared from time to time after taking into consideration the feedback from the various stakeholders such as banks, technology solution providers, members of public and other experts in the field.

6.3 Vision Document for Payment Systems, 2005-08

This Vision Document set out the roadmap for implementing the vision for payment and settlement systems within the next three years. The key themes of the action plans identified in the Vision Document were safety, security, soundness and efficiency (Triple-S and E). While safety in payment and settlement systems related to risk reduction measures, security implied confidence in the integrity of the payment systems. All payment systems were envisaged to be on a sound footing with adequate legal backing for operational procedures and transparency norms. Efficiency enhancements were envisaged by leveraging the benefits of technology for cost effective solutions.

The main action points for Payment and Settlement Systems, 2005-08 as set out in the Vision Document were as indicated below:

6.3.1 Action Points during 2005-06:

1. Pursuing with Indian Banks' Association and major banks

for setting up of a national level entity to operate all retail payment systems in the country.

2. Operationalising National Settlement System for all clearings at four metro centres by December 2005.
3. Finalising the proposed EFT regulations.
4. Implementing Stage-2 of RTGS System, i.e., integrated accounting system (IAS)-RTGS rollout during which all inter-bank transactions at all major centres would be settled on RTGS platform and paper-based inter-bank clearing would be closed.
5. Pursuing with RTGS participants to cover all their networked branches under RTGS framework paving way for RTGS-based customer related transactions at about ten thousand branches in the country.
6. Implementing image-based CTS in the National Capital Region (NCR) on a pilot basis.
7. Preparing minimum standard of operational efficiency at MICR cheque processing centre (CPC).
8. Making available EFT facility at 500 capital market intensive centres as identified by Bombay Stock Exchange (BSE) and National Stock Exchange (NSE).
9. Setting up customer facilitation centre (CFC) at the RBI for various segments of national payment systems.
10. Public disclosure from each payment service provider of its standards, terms and conditions under which the payment would be effected and also compensation policy and procedure for any deficiency in services including the setting up of CFC.
11. Drafting the Red Book on payment systems in India.
12. Drafting a comprehensive legislation on payment system.

6.3.2 Action Points during 2006-07:

1. To complete the tasks initiated during 2005-06.
2. To extend MICR clearing to 20 additional identified centres.
3. To ensure that every cheque issued follows MICR format and standards.

4. To implement EFT system at a national level through the new retail payment institution.
5. To take all payment systems in India compliant with the core principles for systemically important payment systems (SIPS).
6. To increase the reach of payment services by means of tie-up and collaboration with other large coverage entities such as the post offices.
7. To facilitate government payments and receipts through electronic mode.

6.3.3 Action Points during 2007-08:

1. Creating off-city back-up arrangements for large value national payment systems such as RTGS and G-Sec clearing.
2. Making fully functional the new organisation for retail payment systems with all such payment under its umbrella.
3. Regulating various payment systems.
4. Ensuring cheque truncation based clearing at Mumbai, Chennai and Kolkata.
5. Covering National Settlement System at all major clearing houses/clearing organisations in the country.

6.4 Vision Document for Payment Systems, 2012-15

The main focus of the Vision Document for Payments Systems, 2012-15 was to provide a thrust to modern electronic payments that are safe, simple and low-cost for use by all. The document aimed at increasing the share of electronic payment transactions and taking measures towards moving to a less cash society and customer convenience.

The focus of cheque clearing operations in the coming years would be consolidation, rationalisation, centralisation through the implementation of grid-based CTS solution (which is Information Technology Act compliant) across the country by NPCI. The grid-based CTS would usher in a standardised cheque clearing scenario across the country. The issuance of CTS 2010 compliant cheques would facilitate this process. Introduction of user/customer friendly features and increasing the number of settlement cycles in NEFT would be further examined.

6.5 Payment and Settlement Systems in India: Vision 2018

It reiterated the commitment of the RBI to encourage greater use of electronic payments by all sections of society so as to achieve a *less-cash* society. The objective was to facilitate provision of a payment system for the future that combines the much-valued attributes of safety, security and universal reach with technological solutions which enable faster processing, enhanced convenience, and the extraction and use of valuable information that accompanies payments.

6.5.1 Vision Statement: Building best of class payment and settlement systems for a *less-cash* India through responsive regulation, robust infrastructure, effective supervision and customer centricity.

The broad contours of Vision 2018 revolved around the 5Cs:

1. Coverage—by enabling wider access to a variety of electronic payment services.
2. Convenience—by enhancing user experience through ease of use and of products and processes.
3. Confidence—by promoting integrity of systems, security of operations and customer protection.
4. Convergence—by ensuring interoperability across service providers.
5. Cost—by making services cost effective for users as well as service providers.

Vision 2018 focused on four strategic initiatives, viz. responsive regulation, robust infrastructure, effective supervision and customer centricity.

Firstly, RBI, in consultation with all the stakeholders, would continue its efforts to create a regulatory framework to promote twin objectives of enhanced coverage with interoperability of the payments system and convenience with security for the end-users in sync with emerging developments and innovations.

Secondly, to build a robust payments infrastructure in the

country to increase the accessibility, availability, interoperability and security of the payment systems would continue to remain a key objective.

Thirdly, to ensure effectiveness of supervisory mechanisms to strengthen the resilience of the financial market infrastructures (FMIs) and system wide important payment systems (SWIPS) in the country besides setting up appropriate oversight framework for new systems, and augmenting the data reporting and fraud monitoring systems.

Fourthly, to adopt a customer-centric approach to streamline the customer grievance redressal mechanism, focus on building customer awareness and education, and initiate customer protection measures.

6.5.2 Expected Outcomes of Vision 2018: New policies proposed to be framed under Vision 2018 with focus on electronic payments would influence the trends in payment systems in the country. Taking into account the positive developments during the period under Vision 2012-2015, and with the concerted efforts of the government and all other stakeholders like banks, payment system operators, users, etc., Vision 2018 was expected to result in:

1. Continued decrease in the share of paper-based clearing instruments.
2. Consistent growth in individual segments of retail electronic payment systems viz. NEFT, IMPS, card transactions, mobile banking, etc.
3. Increase in registered customer base for mobile banking.
4. Significant growth in acceptance infrastructure.
5. Accelerated use of Aadhaar in payment systems.

6.6 Payment and Settlement Systems in India: Vision 2019-21

RBI's Vision Document on Payment and Settlement Systems, released on May 15, 2019, had the core theme of Empowering Exceptional (E) Payment Experience.

Vision 2021 concentrated on a two-pronged approach of: (a) exceptional customer experience and (b) enabling an ecosystem which would result in this customer experience. With this in view, the Vision aimed towards:

1. Enhancing the experience of customers.
2. Empowering payment system operators and service providers.
3. Enabling the eco-system and infrastructure.
4. Putting in place a forward-looking regulation.
5. Supported by a risk-focussed supervision.

To achieve the above, the Vision envisaged four goal-posts (4 Cs): competition, cost, convenience and confidence.

Significant progress has been made in improving the payment systems infrastructure in India with the introduction of RTGS, operation of high value cheque clearing system (HVCCS), setting up of Clearing Corporation of India Limited (CCIL) as the central counterparty in the government securities, foreign exchange and collateralised borrowing and lending obligation (CBLO) segments as also setting up central counterparties (CCPs) for the settlement of equities and derivatives. The legal framework for payment and settlement systems has also been strengthened by the Payment and Settlement Systems Act, 2007 and the Regulations framed thereunder.

The efficiency of the financial infrastructure—of which the payments and settlement process is a crucial component—is an important factor in promoting financial sector development, improving the effectiveness of monetary policy, and reducing the country risk profile. Integration of the payment services across the country and markets abroad is an important reason for improving the payments system. The development of the payments system is not just a matter of technology. It requires high availability of reliable communication network, the integration of work processes, and delivery systems.

The payment instruments are constantly changing and newer products and services are being innovated in the developed and developing countries and these are being introduced with suitable modifications and safeguards in India. At the retail level a wide range of payment instruments are catering to the needs of different types of economic transactions. At the level of inter-bank payments and settlements, real time and on-line funds transfer are playing a major role both in local as well as inter-city dealings.

To sum up, a smooth and efficient payment and settlement infrastructure plays an important role in maintaining stability in the financial sector. The spread and the reach of the modern system should enable equal and convenient access from both small and big centres alike. The design of an integrated system should be such that there is a wide choice of payments instruments at the retail level and there is end-to-end connectivity throughout the country to enable delivery of these instruments through fast, reliable and secure communications.

An integrated system would enable real time movement of funds between different financial markets, allow fair and equal access to all the financial intermediaries and enable effective regulatory oversight. The fundamental requirement is the integration of various payments instruments, transactions and settlements into a single system which combines flexibility with efficiency. Government is prioritising standard e-payment services such as tax payments, refunds and pension contributions. Welfare payments are also being increasingly digitalised, partly as a means to ensure financial inclusion among poorer segments of the population.

While governments around the world are making great strides in enhancing their e-payment systems, the benchmarks and standards against which they are judged are being raised because of relentless technological and behavioural change.

For e-payments, as with many other new technologies, governments around the world have a responsibility to foster an environment in which citizens, businesses and other stakeholders can feel confident experimenting with and adopting new behaviours and processes.

7

Organizations Linked to Payment Systems

Apart from the Reserve Bank of India (RBI), there are some other organizations which are crucially linked to payment and settlement systems in India.

7.1 Board for Regulation and Supervision of Payment and Settlement Systems (BPSS)

See section 6.2 of chapter 6 of this book.

7.2 Clearing Corporation of India Limited (CCIL)

CCIL was incorporated on April 30, 2001, to provide clearing and settlement services in government securities, foreign exchange and money market instruments. The RBI took the initiative of setting up the CCIL with State Bank of India (SBI), Industrial Development Bank of India (IDBI), Life Insurance Corporation of India (LIC), ICICI Bank Ltd., Bank of Baroda and HDFC Bank Ltd., as its core promoters. This initiative was taken recognising the need for upgrading the country's financial infrastructure in respect of clearing and settlement of debt instruments and forex transactions. CCIL currently provides guaranteed settlement facility for government securities clearing, clearing of collateralised borrowing and lending obligations (CBLO) and foreign exchange clearing.

CCIL-operated systems include the following:

7.2.1 Government Securities Segment: During 1996-2002, a quasi-DvP system was in place with the book-entry system in government securities not directly linked with the funds accounts, with no mechanism to prevent a gridlock in the system. In 2002, CCIL was constituted by the banks to play the role of a CCP and for providing a settlement guarantee mechanism. The government securities settlement system has evolved since then and transactions are now settled on a net basis. Settlement through CCIL has the following advantages: (a) assurance of settlement to the members on the settlement date, (b) reduction in counterparty exposure, (c) operational efficiency, and (d) improved liquidity.

CCIL provides guaranteed settlement of all secondary market outright sales and repo transactions in government securities by the process of novation. All trades reported on the RBI's NDS platform or contracted on the online anonymous, trading platform NDSOM, are accepted by CCIL for settlement after the necessary validations. These trades are settled on a DvP-III basis, i.e. the funds leg and the securities leg are settled on a net basis.

7.2.2 CBLO Segment: The CBLO is a money market product developed by CCIL and launched on January 20, 2003. The product was initially developed with a view to providing entities that have been phased out from the unsecured inter-bank call money market with an avenue for their funds operations. A repo variant, CBLO enables borrowing/lending of funds of various maturities up to one year, fully backed by collaterals in the form of central government securities/treasury bills. CCIL provides guaranteed settlement facility for trades in this instrument as a central counterparty. The funds leg of the trades in this instrument is settled in the current account maintained by these entities with the RBI. The borrowing and lending takes place through an electronic anonymous order matching platform. CBLO operates in a straight-through processing (STP)-enabled environment, seamlessly encompassing dealing to settlement.

The CBLO market has now become the preferred option for participants in the money market. The volume in this market is now significantly higher than the combined volumes in the call and the repo market.

7.2.3 Forex Segment: CCIL provides a guaranteed settlement facility for all US dollar-Indian Rupee inter-bank cash, tom, spot and forward transactions. The matched and accepted forward deals are guaranteed for settlement from S-2 day (two days previous to settlement) and the spot, tom, cash deals are guaranteed for settlement from the trade date as the CCIL becomes the central counterparty to every accepted trade through the process of novation. The rupee-leg of the transaction is settled through the member's current account with the RBI and the US dollar leg through CCIL's account with the Settlement Bank at New York.

CCIL also provides continuous-linked settlement (CLS) settlement services for banks in India by availing of third party services of a settlement bank. Banks participating in this segment of CCIL report their cross-currency trades to the settlement bank directly or through CCIL. The settlement is made through the nostro accounts of CCIL with the settlement bank in CLS settlement currencies.

The settlement of forex transactions by CCIL has resulted in a reduction in counterparty exposure, increased operational efficiency and overall lower operational costs. Forex settlement volumes in CCIL have been rising consistently through the years and have witnessed substantial growth since it commenced operations.

7.3 National Securities Clearing Corporation Ltd (NSCCL)

NSCCL, a wholly-owned subsidiary of NSE, was incorporated in August 1995 and commenced operating as a clearing corporation in April 1996. Clearing and settlement operations of the NSE are managed by NSCCL. It was the first clearing corporation to provide novation/settlement guarantee that revolutionised the entire concept of settlement system in India. It was set up to: (a) bring and sustain confidence in clearing and settlement of securities, (b) promote and maintain short and consistent settlement cycles, (c) provide counterparty risk guarantee, and (d) operate a tight risk containment system.

The settlements of trade in the equities market (both cash and derivative segments) are settled in the BSE by clearing house called BOISL which is a company, jointly promoted by BSE (49 percent) and Bank of India (51 percent). BOISL, *inter alia*, handles some of the settlement-related activities of BSE as per instructions and directions of BSE. Responsibility of the clearing house is to handle such settlement activities including co-ordination with the market participants, viz. depositories, clearing banks etc.

However, the overall responsibility of settlement and risk management functions, viz. collection of margins, collateral management etc. pertaining to transactions done on BSE Online Trading (BOLT) System lies with the BSE.

NSCCL undertakes clearing of transactions executed on the National Stock Exchange for Automated Trading (NEAT) system of NSE. It carries out clearing and settlement functions as per the settlement cycles of different sub-segments in the equities segment. The reforms in the securities settlement systems have resulted in following benefits:

1. Reduction and mitigation of systemic, structural and operational risks.
2. Increase speed of transaction, execution and settlement of trade and quicker settlement of transactions with finality.
3. Safety of the settlement process.
4. Reduction of transaction costs and, thereby, making market more efficient and transparent for investors and participants.

7.4 Government Securities Settlement System

The infrastructure for the government securities settlement systems in India is provided by the RBI. The Public Debt Office (PDO) in the RBI functions as the depository. The PDO has well-laid-down guidelines for opening subsidiary general ledger accounts (SGL) for recording all purchase and sales transactions in government securities. Secondary market transactions in government securities are settled in the books of the RBI for both securities leg and funds leg on delivery versus payment (DvP) basis.

A series of measures taken by the RBI has changed the way the government securities settle currently in India:

1. **July 1995: Introduction of Delivery versus Payment (DvP):** The system was DvP I, wherein securities and funds

were settled on a gross basis. Through this, settlement risk has been greatly reduced.

2. **February 2002: Establishment of Clearing Corporation of India (CCIL):** Acting as a central counterparty through novation, the CCIL provides guaranteed settlement and has put in place risk management systems to limit settlement risk and operates a settlement guarantee fund backed by lines of credit from commercial banks. The netting of funds by CCIL reduces the liquidity requirements of the market and thereby liquidity risk of the system. All the transactions in government securities market, concluded or reported on NDS and NDS-OM have to be necessarily settled through the CCIL.
3. **February 2002: Introduction of Negotiated Dealing System (NDS):** Besides enabling electronic dealing and transparency in the system, the NDS-enabled paperless settlement of transactions in government securities with electronic connectivity to CCIL and the DvP settlement system at the Public Debt Office through electronic SGL transfer form. All entities having SGL Accounts with the RBI were advised to join the NDS-CCIL system by March 31, 2003.
4. **May 2002: Introduction of Compulsory Holding of Government Securities in Demat Form:** Compulsory holding of government securities in demat form for the RBI-regulated entities was introduced to prevent possibility of fraudulent transactions in government securities held in physical form. This improved the efficiency of security settlements by reducing the time taken and aided in simplification of settlement procedures.
5. **March 2004: Introduction of Real Time Gross Settlement System (RTGS):** Introduction of RTGS system was an important measure in improving the stability of settlements in all inter-bank transactions including the government securities. The netted settlement files are also currently being submitted on RTGS for settlement. The system has integrated module for IDL against government securities. Towards the end of 2006, the total solution release (TSR) of RTGS has

been implemented in which the security settlement system (SSS) has been integrated facilitating *on-demand* IDL facility for the market participants.

6. **May 2005: Introduction of Standardised Settlement Cycle of T+1:** The settlement cycle for all outright OTC and NDS-OM trades in government securities was standardised to T+1 cycle for better fund management and risk management by the participants.

7.5 National Payments Corporation of India (NPCI)

NPCI is an umbrella organization for all retail payments system in India. It was set up with the guidance and support of the RBI and Indian Banks' Association (IBA).

The RBI, after setting up the Board for Regulation and Supervision of Payment and Settlement Systems (BPSS) in 2005, released a vision document incorporating a proposal to set up an umbrella institution for all the retail payment systems in the country. The core objective was to consolidate and integrate the multiple systems with varying service levels into nation-wide uniform and standard business process for all retail payment systems. The other objective was to facilitate an affordable payment mechanism to benefit the common man across the country and help financial inclusion.

IBA's untiring efforts helped to turn this vision into a reality. NPCI was incorporated in December 2008 and the Certificate of Commencement of Business was issued in April 2009. It was incorporated as a Section 25 company under the Companies Act, 1956 (now Section 8 of Companies Act, 2013) and is aimed to operate for the benefit of all the member banks and their customers. The aim is to create infrastructure of large dimension and operate on high volumes resulting in payment services at a fraction of the present cost structure.

NPCI has ten core promoter banks, namely State Bank of India, Punjab National Bank, Canara Bank, Bank of Baroda, Union Bank of India, Bank of India, ICICI Bank, HDFC Bank, Citibank and HSBC.

From a single service of switching of inter-bank ATM transactions, the range of services has grown to cheque clearing, immediate payments service (24x7x365), automated clearing house, electronic benefit transfer and a domestic card payment network named RuPay to provide an alternative to international card schemes.

BPSS at its meeting held on September 24, 2009 had given an in-principle approval to issue authorization to NPCI for operating various retail payment systems in the country and granted certificate of authorization for operation of National Financial Switch (NFS) ATM Network with effect from October 15, 2009. NPCI had deputed its officials to IDRBT Hyderabad and had taken over NFS operations on December 14, 2009. Membership regulations and rules had been framed for enrolling all banks in the country as members. This was done so that when the nation-wide payment systems are launched, all would get included on a standardized platform.

One of the more successful products of NPCI has been the unified payments interface (UPI) that powers multiple bank accounts into a single mobile application (of any participating bank) for immediate fund transfers and a variety of payments without parting with sensitive information. It supports merchant payments, utility bill payments, "over-the-counter" payments, QR code (scan and pay)-based payments and the like, through mobile devices on a 365x24x7 basis. The UPI has exhibited significant growth since inception—both in volume and value terms—and has established itself as a veritable conduit for retail funds transfers.

The NPCI symbol uses the acronym of the organization's name. The letter forms are arranged to reflect solidity with progressiveness and dynamism. The use of the red dot and swirl make the entire image unique and memorable. The swirl also communicates worldwide presence. The green and red combination is reminiscent of the Indian National colours. It presents a fresh, individualistic and environmentally conscious message to the world.

The proximate objective behind NPCI is provision of convenient *anytime-anywhere* payment services that are secure and easy-to-use. An attendant goal is to facilitate an affordable payment mechanism to benefit the common person and to catalyse financial inclusion as well. In a span of about a decade of its existence, NPCI has gained the status of being a systemically important payment infrastructure (SIPI).

India has been enjoying a very healthy evolution of payment systems. This has been the result of the calibrated approach adopted by the RBI—in the initial years as a developer, and in later years as a catalyst and facilitator. Today, India's systems are not only comparable to systems anywhere in the world, but they also set standards and good practices for others to emulate.

7.6 National Financial Switch (NFS)

The Institute of Development and Research in Banking Technology (IDRBT), Hyderabad had been providing ATM switching service to banks in India through NFS. NFS network started its operations on August 27, 2004. NFS was one of the several shared ATM networks which inter-connect the ATM switches of the banks together and thus enabled inter-operability of the ATM cards issued by any bank across the entire network.

IDRBT decided to hive off its operational role on ATM switching to have focus on research and development and was looking for a suitable arrangement for shifting this business to some national level payment system organization. National Payments Corporation of India (NPCI) considered this as an opportunity and started discussions with IDRBT on the feasibility of taking over.

The Board for Regulation and Supervision of Payment and Settlement systems (BPSS) at its meeting held on September 24, 2009 approved in-principle to issue authorisation to NPCI for operating various retail payment systems in the country. Reserve Bank of India (RBI) also issued authorisation to NPCI to take over the operations of NFS from IDRBT on *as is where is basis* on October 15, 2009. NPCI took over NFS operations from

December 14, 2009.

7.7 National Automated Clearing House (NACH)

National Payments Corporation of India (NPCI) has implemented National Automated Clearing House (NACH) for banks, financial institutions, corporates and Government. It is a web-based solution to facilitate inter-bank, high volume, electronic transactions which are repetitive and periodic in nature. NACH system can be used for making bulk transactions towards distribution of subsidies, dividends, interest, salary, pension etc. and also for bulk transactions towards collection of payments pertaining to telephone, electricity, water, loans, investments in mutual funds, insurance premium etc.

NACH is a centralised system aimed at consolidating multiple electronic clearing services (ECS) systems running across the country. It provides a framework for the harmonization of standards and practices and removes local barriers/inhibitors. NACH system provides a national footprint and covers the entire core banking enabled bank branches spread across the geography of the country irrespective of the location of the bank branch.

With the implementation of NACH system, NPCI intends to provide a single set of rules (operating and business), open standards and best industry practices for electronic transactions which are common across all the participants, service providers and users etc. NACH system also supports financial inclusion measures initiated by Government, Government agencies and banks by providing support to Aadhaar-based transactions.

NACH system facilitates the member banks to design their own products and also addresses specific needs of the banks and corporates including a refined mandate management system (MMS) and an online dispute management system (DMS) coupled with strong information exchange and customised MIS capabilities.

NACH system provides a robust, secure and scalable platform to the participants with both transaction and file based transaction processing capabilities. It has best in class security features, cost efficiency and payment performance coupled with multi-level data validation facility accessible to all participants across the country.

NACH's Aadhaar Payment Bridge (APB) system, developed by NPCI has been helping the Government and Government agencies in making the Direct Benefit Transfer (DBT) scheme a success. APB system has been successfully channelizing the Government subsidies and benefits to the intended beneficiaries using the Aadhaar numbers. APB system links the Government departments and their sponsor banks on one side and beneficiary banks and beneficiary on the other side.

A variant of NACH called eNACH has been created, which is digital, and relies on a digital signature of the user (based on eSign with Aadhaar). This is convenient because it simplifies the process of on-boarding a new customer (no issues with checking a wet signature). Recently, the RBI approved the use of other authentication methods for eNach, including net banking, and debit card.

7.8 Committee to Review the Framework Related to Digital Payments

Ministry of Finance, Government of India had constituted this Committee on Digital Payments to review the payment systems in the country and to recommend appropriate measures for encouraging digital payments. The Committee (Chairman: Ratan P. Watal) was constituted on August 23, 2016 with the following terms of reference:

1. To study and recommend need for charges, if any, in the regulatory mechanism and any legislation, relevant for the purpose of promotion of payments by digital modes.
2. To study and recommend ways for leveraging Unique Identification Number or any other proof of identity for authentication of card/digital transactions and setting up of a Centralised KYC Registry.
3. To study introduction of single window system of Payment

Gateway to accept all types of cards/digital payments of Government receipts.

4. To study feasibility and framing rules for creating a payments history of all digital payments and create necessary linkages between payments transaction history and credit information.
5. To study and recommend various measures to incentivize transactions through cards and digital means.
6. To study global best practices in payments including initiatives taken by various Governments/Government agencies.
7. To identify market failure(s), if any, along with suitable interventions that may be implemented to promote payment by card/digital means.
8. To identify regulatory bottlenecks, if any, and suggest changes to promote payment by card/digital means.
9. To study and make recommendations on any other matter related to promotion of payments through cards and digital means.

The Committee submitted an Interim Report to the Ministry of Finance on November 21, 2016. Towards finalization of the report, the Committee engaged extensively with all stakeholders and technology groups including the RBI, State Governments, Comptroller and Auditor General of India, payment companies, technology companies and the academia. The Committee submitted its Final Report to the Finance Minister on December 9, 2016.

The Committee, *inter alia*, recommended a medium-term strategy for accelerating growth of digital payments in India with a regulatory regime which is conducive to bridging the *digital divide* by promoting competition, open access and inter-operability in payments. The Committee recommended inclusion of financially and socially excluded groups and assimilation of emerging technologies in the market, while safeguarding security of digital transactions and providing level playing to all stakeholders and new players who will enter this new transaction space. It suggested inter-operability of the payments system between banks and non-banks, upgradation of the digital payment infrastructure and institutions and a framework to reward innovations and for leading efforts in enabling digital payments.

The Committee was seized of the developments following the decision of the Government to cancel legal tender character of currency of high denominations. The Committee calibrated its recommendations accordingly and provided a suitable framework for smooth and speedy transition towards a digital payments economy.

8

Paper-based Traditional Systems of Payment

Due to steps taken by the RBI to encourage electronic transactions, paper-based systems constitute a miniscule portion of retail payments. The number of clearing houses has also declined.

Negotiable Instruments (NI) Act, 1881, defines a negotiable instrument as a promissory note, bill of exchange or cheque. A bill of exchange is an instrument in writing containing an unconditional order, signed by the maker, directing a certain person to pay a certain sum of money only to, or to the order of, a certain person or to the bearer of the instrument. A *hundi* is a bill of exchange in an Indian language, governed by customs and local usage. The NI Act, however, does not govern *hundis*. A bill of exchange may therefore, include a *hundi*, but *hundi* may not be a bill of exchange.

8.1 Cheque

A cheque is a bill of exchange drawn on a specified banker and not expressed to be payable otherwise than on demand. The maker of a cheque is called the *drawer*, and the person directed to pay is the *drawee*. The person named in the instrument, to whom or to whose order the money is, by the instrument directed, to be paid, is called the *payee*. A cheque is a negotiable instrument, which can be further negotiated by means of endorsement and is payable on demand. A cheque payable to bearer is negotiable by the delivery thereof, and when it is payable to order is negotiable by the holder by endorsement and delivery thereof. A cheque has to be presented for payment by the payee or holder to the acceptor, maker or drawer. A cheque payment is a debit transaction as the transaction regarding the payment of a cheque is initiated by the payee or beneficiary.

A cheque is not cash, as it does not assume the finality of payment. The funds may not be available with the drawer or the drawer may have withdrawn funds from his bank account in the interim leading to the possibility of the cheque being dishonoured on presentation. In addition, the banks levy a collection charge based on postal costs as well as the value of the cheque in case of outstation cheques. It takes time to realise the proceeds of a cheque payment, especially if the cheque is an outstation one. For these reasons, the cheque is not always acceptable in several business transactions particularly where the drawer and the payee are not known to each other. In many commercial transactions, the sellers of goods and services prefer to have a payment instrument where the sum of money payable to the payee is guaranteed. The demand draft is one such instrument.

As the business activities are expanding, cheque volumes have also increased, particularly in the commercial and financial hubs of the country. As a result of the financial inclusion policy of the Government, cheque transactions are also becoming popular in rural areas.

RBI has advised banks to align their policies with the objective of financial inclusion. Banks have been advised to make available a basic banking *no frills* account either with *nil* or very minimum balances as well as charges that would make such accounts accessible to vast sections of population. Besides, RBI has emphasized for deepening and widening the reach of financial services so as to cover a large segment of the rural and poor sections of population.

All the public and the private sector banks as well as the foreign banks, except those not having significant retail presence, are reported to have introduced the basic banking *no-frills* account.

In view of the expanding volume of cheques, efforts have been made to switch over from manual sorting and listing of instruments to more efficient and electronically-driven systems.

8.1.1 Clearing Infrastructure: There are both direct members and sub-members in a clearing house. All the branches of a member bank within the clearing house jurisdiction have the right to present and receive cheques drawn on any other member bank or branch within the same jurisdiction. The sub-members are sponsored by a member bank. They can participate in clearing operations in the same way as a branch of a member bank.

The dominant feature of the Indian banking system is its branch-cantered banking. The vast network of branches implies that the logistics of collection and delivery of paper payment instruments becomes formidable. The clearing infrastructure is designed to address the movement of instruments between the presenting and drawee branches. Each member bank in a centre is represented in the clearing house by its service branch which collects all the instruments from various branches and consolidates them for presentation to all the banks in the clearing house. Similarly, it receives and distributes among its branches all the instruments drawn upon its branches by other banks in the clearing house. The service branch of a bank performs a crucial intermediary role between the clearing house and the branch of a bank.

The clearing process starts with the deposit of a cheque (through pay-in-slip) in a bank. The cheque is delivered to the bank on which it is drawn. The cheque is cleared for payment if the funds are available and the bank is satisfied that the cheque is genuine. Unpaid cheques are returned to the presenting bank through another clearing called the return clearing. Realisation of the funds is affected only after the completion of return clearing and by the absence of any pending unpaid cheque.

The settlement of funds in clearing occurs at several levels. The aggregate amount or value of cheques presented by a bank on other banks represents the claim by that bank on other banks. Similar claims are made by all the banks on every other bank in the clearing. A net settlement is arrived at the clearing house and the debit or credit position of the bank is determined. These are booked in their current accounts maintained by the settling bank. This represents the inter-bank settlement. The settlement of funds between the service branch and the branch concerned represents the transfer of funds to the branch level. The payment process is completed only when the funds are debited from the drawer's account and credited to the payee's account. This occurs after the completion of the return clearing.

The complete clearing cycle—inclusive of return clearing—causes a time lag in the payments process. Physical presentment of the cheque at the bank branch, where it is drawn on, requires the movement of cheques from one place to another. Thus, the recipient of payment has to wait until the collecting bank is satisfied that the cheque has been honoured. So long as the physical presentment of the cheque is necessary as per the banking law, this time lag is likely to continue irrespective of the level of technology and upgradation of the process.

As the clearing jurisdiction is local, a separate procedure has evolved for the collection of cheques drawn on banks outside the clearing house area. In this case, the cheques are sent by post for collection to the representative branch or correspondent branch for presentation in the clearing house in the outstation centre. Once the cheque is realised, the proceeds are remitted to the original presenting bank for credit to the customer account. This leads to a significant delay in the payment of these cheques and there is considerable uncertainty regarding the time of realisation.

Prior to 1986, there were no formal regulations and rules governing the transaction of business in the clearing houses. Each Clearing House had its own rules and regulations based on local conventions and convenience. In case of disputes, problem resolution proved to be a tricky exercise.

In 1986, Reserve Bank of India framed a set of guidelines known as the Uniform Regulations and Rules (URR) for the Bankers' Clearing Houses. These guidelines were prescribed against the backdrop of considerable changes occurring in the functioning of the clearing houses due to the introduction of computerisation in the banking industry.

Regulations are designed to provide a uniform framework for the conduct of clearing throughout the country and have been adopted individually by the general body of each clearing house in the country. Individual clearing houses are free to frame their own rules consistent with the broad framework provided by the Regulations.

URR represents a significant step forward in providing a formal institutional framework for the payments system in the country. They govern the conduct of the clearing business, prescribe fair membership criteria and provide for penalties in the case of default. They also explicitly provide for significant oversight function for the Reserve Bank of India.

8.1.2 Computerisation of Clearing and Settlement Operations: Computerisation of clearing operations was the first major step towards modernisation of the payments system. The introduction of technology for clearing operations began with the setting up of claim-based settlement system using micro processor-based computer systems at Mumbai, Chennai and Delhi, in the early 1980s. These systems were used for generating settlement reports on the basis of input statements containing the aggregate value of (cheques presented) claims of one bank over the other banks in the clearing house. Clearing balancing and settlement, which used to take a long time due to differences and errors in manual balancing, were reduced, apart from providing accuracy in the final settlement.

The next important milestone was fully automating the clearing operations. The rapid growth of cheque volumes in the eighties made the task of manual sorting and listing a very difficult task. Banks were unable to cope with the huge volume of cheques which had to be physically handled prior to their presentation in the clearing house. Though the clearing settlement became easy because of computerisation, the heavy volumes of paper that had to be processed, introduced delays in presentation resulting in delayed credit to the customers. The growth in the volumes could therefore, be managed only by mechanisation of the entire clearing process. The solution was the introduction of MICR.

8.1.3 Magnetic Ink Character Recognition (MICR): With the introduction of MICR-based mechanised cheque processing technology, the existing cheques had to be redesigned incorporating a MICR code which could be read by document processing machines called reader-sorters. The magnetic media-based input settlement represented an intermediate step towards complete automation of cheque clearing through MICR processing and enabled banks and the clearing house to get accustomed to a computerised environment.

MICR cheque processing was replaced by cheque truncation system (CTS).

8.1.4 Cheque Truncation System (CTS): The introduction of CTS was a step for increasing the efficiency of retail payment system.

A. What is CTS? Truncation is the process of stopping the flow of the physical cheque issued by a drawer to the drawee branch. The physical instrument is truncated at some point enroute to the drawee branch and an electronic image of the cheque is sent to the drawee branch along with the relevant information like the MICR fields, date of presentation, presenting banks etc. Thus, with the implementation of cheque truncation, the need to move the physical instruments across branches is not required, except in exceptional circumstances. This has effectively reduced the time required for payment of cheques, the associated cost of transit and delay in processing, etc., thus speeding up the process of collection or realization of the cheques.

B. CTS Implementation: RBI implemented CTS in the National Capital Region (NCR), New Delhi, Chennai and Mumbai with effect from February 1, 2008, September 24, 2011 and April 27, 2013 respectively. After migration of the entire cheque volume from MICR system to CTS, the traditional MICR-based cheque processing was discontinued in the country. Based on the advantages realised by the stakeholders and the experience gained from the roll-out in these centres, it was decided to operationalise CTS across the country.

The new approach, envisioned as part of the national roll-out, is grid-based. Under this approach, the entire cheque volume in the country, which was earlier cleared through 66 MICR cheque processing locations, is consolidated into the three grids in New Delhi, Chennai and Mumbai. Each grid provides processing and clearing services to all the banks under its respective jurisdiction. Under grid-based cheque truncation system clearing, all cheques drawn on bank branches falling within in the grid jurisdiction are treated and cleared as local cheques.

C. Advantages of CTS: To wish away cheques is simply not possible and that is the reason why RBI decided to focus on improving the efficiency of the cheque clearing cycle.

Cheque truncation speeds up collection of cheques and therefore enhances customer service, reduces scope for clearing related frauds, minimizes cost of collection of cheques, reduces reconciliation problems, eliminates logistics problems etc.

Moreover, contrary to perceptions, cheque truncation is a more secure system than the current exchange of physical documents in which the cheque moves from one point to another, thus, not only creating delays but inconvenience to the customer in case the instrument is lost in transit or manipulated during the clearing cycle.

Besides operational efficiency, cheque truncation has various benefits for banks and customers which, *inter alia*, include introduction of new products, re-designing the total receipts and payments mechanism of the customers, human resource rationalization, cost effectiveness etc. Therefore, cheque truncation is a significant efficiency enhancement initiative undertaken by RBI in the payment systems area.

8.2 Other Paper-based Instruments of Payment

8.2,1 Demand Draft: It is a pre-paid negotiable instrument stating that the drawee bank undertakes to make payment in full when the instrument is presented by the payee for payment. It is payable on a specified branch of a bank at a specified centre. To receive payment, the beneficiary has to either present the instrument directly to the bank branch concerned or to get it collected though his/her bank by the clearing mechanism.

8.2.2 Banker's Cheque: It is another payment instrument used by banks to settle payment obligations on behalf of their customers. Bankers's cheque is guaranteed by the bank for its full value and is similar to a demand draft. In fact, these instruments are payable at the branch of issue and used for making payment within the local clearing jurisdiction.

8.2.3 Payment Orders: Payment orders are issued by banks for payments made on behalf of the bank. These instruments are signed by a banker and carry the guarantee of the bank on the availability of the funds. These instruments are payable at the branch of issue.

8.2.4 Travellers Cheques: Carrying large amounts of cash is very risky, especially when one is travelling. Travellers' cheques are a secure and convenient alternative to carrying cash. These are pre-paid instruments available in fixed denominations. The holder of the travellers' cheque is required to sign the instrument upon purchase and again in the presence of the merchant establishment at the time of making payment or realising proceeds thereof. Travellers' cheques can be replaced if they are lost or stolen at no additional cost. Travellers' cheques are available in both domestic and international currency. These instruments can be readily exchanged at bank branches anywhere and in several merchant establishments.

8.2.5 Interest Warrant: It is issued for payment of periodic interest on fixed deposits with companies as well as government securities. It is a special type of cheque which is *payable at par* at various branches of a bank across the country. The term *at par* means that the full-face value of the instrument has to be credited to the account of the payee, without resorting to any deductions in the form of collection charges, which banks generally levy whenever an instrument is sent for collection. It is noteworthy that dividend warrants are similar to the interest warrants and are usually payable *at par* to the shareholders of a company.

Interest warrants have a long history coinciding with the servicing of public debt. In India, servicing of public debt (i.e. payment of interest to holders of Government securities) is done by the Public Debt Office of the RBI, which issues interest warrants, payable *at par* at all offices of RBI and State Bank of India.

8.2.6 Dividend Warrants: Joint stock companies issue interest or dividend warrants and refund orders with a prior funding arrangement with a bank. A company funds an account with its bank with a sum equal to at least the total value of the interest warrants to be issued. The bank provides *at par* facility whereby an instrument drawn on that particular bank is payable at par in selected branches of the bank as also the branches of the correspondent bank at various locations across the country. These warrants are honoured by the paying branches debiting the funding account of the company.

Corporate clients are also extended the facility to issue current account cheques *at par* by their bankers on a very selective basis. This is largely done to facilitate payments to upcountry suppliers and others. Similarly, for payments from retailers and other upcountry buyers of corporate products, banks offer collection accounts facilities to reputed companies. The payments to the company are channelled through special accounts throughout the country and repatriated to the headquarters' account.

The payment instruments described above are all paper-based and require to be tendered at specific banks for payment either in person or through another bank in clearing or through collection. Under the NI Act, 1881, the cheque or the instrument has to be presented to the drawer. The chief disadvantage with the cheque and the demand draft is that these instruments have to be physically presented, often leading to delays in payment. To overcome delays, fund transfers through the medium of telex were introduced. The telegraphic transfers represent payment instructions sent in a telex mode to an upcountry branch of the same bank or to a correspondent bank branch to credit the beneficiary's account with a given amount. A cipher code is appended to the text of the message to ensure its integrity and authenticity during transit.

8.2.7 Money Order: Money order service is offered by the Department of Posts, Government of India. The money order enables an individual to send remittances to a third party under the aegis of the post office. It is a point-to-point delivery of funds. The originating post office collects the full amount of remittance as also a commission (service charge) from the individual remitting the funds and sends the advice to the destination post office. At the destination post office, the funds are paid to the beneficiary. The money order can be sent as an ordinary paper-based payment advice or as a *telegraphic money order*. The telegraphic money order is faster as the payment advices are sent through telex or telegraph. The customer, of course, has to pay higher service charges for this facility.

The postal order is another payment instrument of the Department of Posts. The postal order is issued denomination-wise, which can be encashed by the beneficiary after due identification at the post office on which it is drawn. Postal orders like the money orders are independent of the banking system.

To sum up, use of paper-based clearing instruments (like cheques and drafts) has been steadily decreasing over a period of time and electronic mode has gained popularity due to the concerted efforts of the RBI to popularize the electronic payment products in preference to cash and cheques. Since paper-based payments occupy an important place in the country, RBI had introduced MICR technology which has now been replaced by cheque truncation system (CTS) for speeding up and bringing in efficiency in processing of cheques.

India has a very efficient clearing house infrastructure, which is used by businesses to clear cheques, across the country, settling them on the same day, or the next day, and is the preferred mode for a lot of business transactions. Most banks do not charge retail customers for cheque clearing.

The clearing and settlement of cheques drawn on different banks require the coming together of the banks in that area for transfer of instruments and the final settlement of funds. This process is facilitated by the clearing houses at various centres. The clearing and settlement cycle is completed in two days—on day 1, the cheques are presented at the clearing house and on day 2, the funds settlement and return clearing are accounted for.

Recent developments in paper-based instruments include launch of speed clearing (for local clearance of outstation cheques drawn on core-banking enabled branches of banks), introduction of cheque truncation system [CTS] (to restrict physical movement of cheques and enable use of images for payment processing), framing CTS-2010 Standards (for enhancing the security features on cheque forms) and the like.

While the overall thrust is to reduce the use of paper for transactions, given the fact that it would take some time to completely move to the electronic mode, the intention is to reduce the movement of paper—both for local and outstation clearance of cheques.

9

Electronic Payments (E-payments) and India's Global Ranking

9.1 What are E-payments?

E-payments are defined as the exchange or transfer of funds over an electronic payment system. Payments through these electronic platforms can be made by various means, including but not limited to payment card, e-wallet, direct deposit, direct debit, electronic funds transfer and wire transfer. The payment component is only one part of the e-payments process, which can also include online submission of forms and the provision of online instructions or calculators to facilitate the use of an e-payments system.

Electronic IDs refer to secure digital identifications provided to individuals as part of a national digital identification system or programme. Examples may include biometric enrolment, microprocessor-based smart card technologies or a username or password for online government portals, among other electronic identification-related technologies.

9.2 Advantages of Electronic Transactions

1. Convenience and ease of transaction.
2. More secure as compared to transactions involving cash.
3. Modernisation of payment system.
4. Transparency and accountability.
5. Reduction in transaction costs.
6. Decrease in the size of the grey or informal economy.
7. Help to business people to expand their customer base beyond the limitations of their immediate geographic area.
8. Environmentally desirable as no trees will be cut for printing paper money. Reduction in corruption.

9.3 E-payment Ranking Survey

The 2018 Government E-Payments Adoption Ranking (GEAR) was an Economist Intelligence Unit (EIU) global index and benchmarking study commissioned by Visa. This was the third edition of the study. The first and second editions were published in 2007 and 2011, respectively.

The objective of the study was to measure the extent to which countries enable payment services on electronic platforms. This included the availability of government transaction services, and the underlying factors that affect e-payments adoption, such as policy and infrastructure.

The overall score and category scores in this benchmarking index were on a normalised scale of 0-100 and represented how countries rank against one another.

The 2018 GEAR study captured some of the essential changes occurring in the worlds of finance and technology, on which developed countries could focus their efforts to advance their government e-payment systems.

The survey looked at availability of government electronic transaction services and the underlying environment of mechanisms that support digitization for all transactions in a market, such as policy and infrastructure.

The 7 categories and 45 indicators researched in the 2018 GEAR survey are listed in Table 9.1.

The first four categories of the index examined the availability of certain government payment services. These measured the availability of e-payment facilities, and not whether they were actually used. The other three categories—infrastructure, social and economic context and policy context—examined the underlying factors that affected adoption of those e-payment facilities.

It is worth reiterating that the transaction services focused on here were government e-payments (where the state is either a payer or a payee), which was a segment of the much broader payments universe.

Table 9.1: Categories and Indicators of the E-payments Survey

1	Citizen-to-Government (C2G) [1]
1.1	Payments platform functionality for transaction Services
1.2	Income tax payments
1.3	Pension contributions
1.4	Obtaining/paying for an ID card
1.5	Private transit costs
1.6	Public transit payments
2	**Government-to-Citizen (G2C) [2]**
2.1	Income tax refunds
2.2	Pension benefits
2.3	Unemployment benefits
2.4	Government social safety net
3	**Business-to-Government (B2G) [3]**
3.1	Business income tax payments
3.2	VAT/sales tax payments
3.3	Business pension contributions
3.4	Company registration and payment of fees
4	**Government-to-Business (G2B) [4]**
4.1	Business income tax refunds
4.2	VAT/sales tax refunds
4.3	Payments for goods and services
4.4	Disbursement of loans
5	**Infrastructure**
5.1.1	Fixed-line broadband subscribers
5.1.2	Active mobile broadband subscribers
5.1.3	Mobile subscribers
5.1.4	Network coverage (minimum 4G)
5.1.5	Government initiatives to make wi-fi available
5.1.6	Existence of national digital identification system
5.2.1	Automatic teller machines (ATMs) per 10,000 people

contd...

5.2.2	Point-of-sale (PoS) terminals per 10,000 people
5.2.3	Development of contactless payments
6	**Social and Economic Context**
6.1.1	Educational attainment
6.1.2	Internet access
6.2.1	Population using banks/other financial institutions
6.2.2	Percentage of firms with a bank loan/line of credit
6.3.1	Proportion of businesses placing orders via the internet
6.3.2	Internet shoppers as a percentage of internet users
6.3.3	Percentage of population with debit card(s)
6.3.4	Used a mobile phone or the internet to access an account
7	**Policy Context**
7.1.1	Fair competition in the payments industry
7.1.2	Policy on acceptance and usage of e-payments
7.1.3	Protection of intellectual property rights
7.1.4	Access to jurisdictions
7.1.5	Government support for FinTech innovation
7.2.1	Government commitment to e-payments security
7.2.2	Government commitment to the Financial Action Task Force (FATF)
7.3.1	Government commitment to integrating the informal Economy
7.3.2	Existence of government e-inclusion strategy
7.3.3	Government commitment to financial inclusion

9.3.1 India in the Overall Rankings: The overall rankings and scores of top 10 countries along with India, China and Pakistan are presented in Table 9.2. The overall score is a weighted sum of category scores (on a 0-100 scale where 100 is the most favourable). The overall scores reflect the enabling environment for government e-payments adoption.

In the 73-country survey, India's overall ranking on the

government's adoption of e-payments moved up to 28th in 2018, from 36th in 2011. The survey noted that India was taking rapid strides in advancing government e-payments capabilities and was one of the top-performing countries in terms of citizen-to-government (C2G), business-to-government (B2G) and government-to-business (G2B) transactions. The country held the top ranking on B2G and G2B, and came third on C2G jointly with Argentina. The survey found that India could further improve its standing by focusing on expanding access to digital infrastructure, investing in socio-economic development, and promoting a healthy, competitive market.

Table 9.2: Overall Ranking and Scores of Top Ten Countries Plus India, China and Pakistan

Rank	Country	Score
1.	Norway	89.7
2.	France	89.4
3.	Denmark	88.8
4.	Canada	88.6
5.	Australia	88.1
6.	United Kingdom	87.9
7.	South Korea	87.7
8.	Singapore	87.6
9.	Finland	86.2
10.	Sweden	85.8
28.	**India**	**73.3**
48.	**China**	**62.4**
64.	**Pakistan**	**47.0**

Source: Economist Intelligence Unit, *Government E-payments Adoption Ranking Report, September 2018*, p. 17 (excerpted).

9.3.2 Other Main Findings of the Survey: These were as under:

1. Government E-payments Adoption Ranking (GEAR) showed that most governments were prioritising the

availability of electronic transaction services for citizens and businesses, albeit at different levels, but that they had significant work to do in improving three areas that support e-payments adoption, namely infrastructure, social and economic context, and policy.

2. The operating environment for government e-payments had changed significantly in the past decade, and there was much room for growth in terms of availability of services and efficiency. The global payments ecosystem was almost unrecognisable from that which existed at the time of the last GEAR in 2011, particularly in terms of the worldwide growth that had taken place in the availability of e-payment mechanisms.
3. While few developing countries featured at the top of the rankings, the seminal trend of these past few years was the continued leapfrogging to more advanced platforms and technologies by emerging markets.
4. Developed countries, on the other hand, where many advances in technology and transaction services had already reached completion, could focus on boosting adoption of systems that had already been enabled while also improving user experiences. At the same time, they needed to decide which of the multitude of available new technologies they wish to experiment with. Blockchain-based identity verification and transactions, for instance, appeared promising, but it was unclear whether their marginal short-term benefits would justify significant investments, particularly for cash-strapped governments.
5. Although it seemed that technology's democratising and decentralising forces were liberating individuals to operate beyond the ambit of the state, the reality was that government policy had never been more important. Countries with proactive governments were the ones that were fostering an enabling environment for fintechs, ensuring financial inclusion and, more generally, striking the appropriate balance between regulatory oversight and innovations.

6. Government e-payment systems had evolved significantly since the first GEAR study in 2007, and yet in some ways the journey was just beginning.

Endnotes

1. **Citizen-to-Government (C2G):** Citizens make regular payments to the state either to fulfil obligations, such as taxes, or to purchase optional public services, including transportation. This category captures the extent to which citizens can complete these various transactions electronically by assessing six indicators: online one-stop shops; income tax payments; pension contributions; obtaining/paying for an ID card; private transit costs (a composite of automotive tolls, fines, vehicle registration and public parking); and public transit payments.
2. **Government-to-Citizen (G2C):** Governments need to make regular payments to certain segments of the population to fulfil core responsibilities such as providing a social safety net. This category captures the extent to which various government transfers to citizens can be completed electronically, by assessing four indicators: income tax refunds, pension benefits, unemployment benefits and the government social safety net.
3. **Business-to-Government (B2G):** Businesses typically make payments to the state for one of three reasons: to fulfil national obligations, such as taxes; as a form of indirect payment to their employees, such as pension contributions; or for direct business costs, including licence fees. The B2G category captures the extent to which businesses can complete these various transactions electronically by assessing four indicators: income tax payments, value-added/sales tax payments, pension contributions, and company registration and payment of fees.
4. **Government-to-Business (G2B):** The state typically makes payments to businesses for one of three reasons: to refund excessive tax collection, to pay for goods and services purchased, or to disburse small grants or loans to spur business activity. This category captures the extent to which various government transfers to businesses can be completed electronically, by assessing four indicators: income tax refunds, VAT/sales tax refunds, payments for goods and services, and the disbursement of loans.

10

Card-based Electronic Payment Systems

Cards are well understood products at the global level, and find acceptance at stores, as well as for online payments. Cards have played an important role in the spread of digital payments. Cards are also used to withdraw money from ATMs, and hence have been issued to most account holders. India has had the presence of international players in the payments space for many years. Recently, an Indian player—National Payments Corporation of India (NPCI)—has also introduced card payments through the RuPay scheme.

Cards are usually issued by banks and can be classified on the basis of their issuance, usage and payment by the card holder. There are three types of cards:

1. Pre-paid cards.
2. Debit cards.
3. Credit cards.

10.1 Pre-paid Cards

These are pre-loaded from a customer's bank account and are equivalent to cash. These can be used for limited amount of transaction and can be recharged several times like mobile recharge. Such cards are safe to use. Pre-paid instruments are payment instruments that facilitate purchase of goods and services against the value stored on these instruments. The value stored on such instruments represents the value paid for by the holders by cash, by debit to a bank account, or by credit card. The pre-paid payment instruments can be issued in the form of smart cards, magnetic stripe cards, internet accounts, internet wallets, mobile accounts, mobile wallets, paper vouchers etc. Pre-paid cards can be used at any point-of-sale (PoS).

Subsequent to the notification of the Payment and Settlement

Systems (PSS) Act, 2007, policy guidelines for issuance and operation of pre-paid instruments in India were issued in the public interest to regulate the issue of pre-paid payment instruments in the country.

The use of pre-paid payment instruments for cross border transactions has not been permitted, except for the payment instruments approved under Foreign Exchange Management Act (FEMA), 1999.

10.2 Debit Cards

A debit card is a plastic payment card that can be used instead of cash when making purchases. Debit card is issued by the bank where a client has an account. Linked to the bank account, debit cards are issued to account holders and any expenditure made is immediately debited to user's account. User can use this card to withdraw cash up to the limit prescribed by the bank. Debit cards can be used only for domestic fund transfer from one person to another.

To complete transaction via debit/credit card, the card is swiped at the card reader (PoS), amount is entered followed by a PIN to be manually punched in by the card holder. Upon authentication the receipt is generated and payment completed.

10.2.1 Types of Debit Card Transactions: Debit card transactions can be accomplished through PIN debit (requires the consumer to enter a PIN), signature debit (no PIN required), online bill payment and online debit. Debit card transactions are the fastest growing point-of-sale payment method today. The acceptance of this payment method continues to remain popular because customers and merchants both appreciate the convenience and ease of using debit cards to purchase merchandise and services.

10.2.2 Personal Identification Number (PIN) Debit and Signature Debit: These two debit choices differ in the sense whether a PIN is used at the point-of-sale (PoS) or not. When a PIN is used, the payment is immediately withdrawn from the cardholder's available funds. When a signature debit transaction occurs, funds are not withdrawn until the transaction processes, usually 2 to 4 days after the sale.

10.3 Credit Cards

A credit card is a payment card issued to users (cardholders) to enable the cardholder to pay a merchant for goods and services, based on the cardholder's promise to the card issuer to pay them for the amounts so paid plus other agreed charges. The card issuer (usually a bank) creates a revolving account and grants a line of credit to the cardholder, from which the cardholder can borrow money for payment to a merchant or as a cash advance.

These are issued by banks and other entities approved by the Reserve Bank of India (RBI). Such cards can be used domestically and internationally (provided it is enabled for international use). Unlike debit cards, in case of credit cards, a customer can withdraw money beyond the amount present in his account. However, there is a limit, for each credit card, up to which extra money can be withdrawn. Also, there is a time limit up to which the extra money withdrawn should be paid back. This amount of money is paid back to the bank along with interest charges, in case of delays beyond the specified period.

There has been phenomenal increase in the number of credit cards issued by the banks in India during the last few years. The number of outstanding credit cards at end-May 2022 stood at over 7.68 crore.

While the increasing usage of the credit cards is a welcome development in as much as it reduces reliance on currency for settlement of transactions, it also entails certain additional elements of operational risk and can be a potential source of customer complaints.

10.4 How to Use Debit/Credit Cards?

To withdraw money from an ATM, user needs to insert his/her debit/credit card and type in the unique PIN number (4 digits) provided by the bank. The maximum amount that can be withdrawn per day is set by the bank. With debit card, a user can also use the ATM to carry out other financial and non-financial transactions such as finding out bank balance, getting a mini statement etc. without visiting the bank branch.

While shopping at retail stores and shops, he/she should follow the following steps.

1. User gives the debit card to the cashier at the store.
2. Cashier runs the card through PoS machine.
3. Cashier types in the amount of the purchase.
4. User types in the PIN of the card.
5. Bank debits (deducts) the amount of purchase directly from user's account.
6. Machine prints out a receipt which has to be signed by the user.
7. Cashier keeps the signed receipt and hands a copy to the user for record.
8. User gets SMS on his registered mobile for transaction completed.

10.5 Benefits of Debit/Credit Cards

These are as under:

1. Debit/credit cards can be used to withdraw cash from ATM, purchase goods and services at point-of-sale (PoS) and purchase online.
2. These cards can be used to pay all kinds of utility bills.
3. Holder can book tickets of airlines, railways and road transport services.
4. Accommodation at hotels can be booked and payments at restaurants can be made.
5. Payment can be made for any service at any location where there is a card reader/PoS machine.

10.5.1 How to Get a Card? A person desirous of obtaining a debit/credit card should apply for the same at his/her respective bank branch. Persons who do not have bank account must first open an account with a bank.

10.6 Automated Teller Machines (ATMs)

Stand-alone ATMs made their appearance in India in early

1990s. These were mostly installed by foreign banks in their branch premises, as per the then existing policy. Easing of restrictions on the location of ATMs has led to their being installed at convenient places such as airports, central business districts, hospitals etc.

ATMs are primarily used for performing some of the banking functions such as withdrawal of cash or deposit of cash/cheque etc., by using an ATM card. Each customer is provided with an ATM card with a unique personal identification number (PIN) of 4 digits. Whenever a customer performs a transaction, the person has to key in the PIN which is validated by the ATM, before the machine permits any transaction. The PIN has to be kept secret by the customer, to prevent any misuse or fraudulent transactions in the event of loss of the card.

The main advantage of an ATM network is that it obviates the need for having bank-specific multiple ATM installations in the same geographical area, thereby reducing the entailed costs for the banks but without compromising on the reach of the banks to their customers.

Over the years, the relative growth in off-site ATMs has been much more than that of on-site ATMs. As a result, by end-May 2022, off-site ATMs accounted for approximately 44.89 percent (97,809) of the total ATMs in the country. With the policy initiative to enable non-bank entities to set up and operate ATMs—White Label ATMs (WLAs)—the proportion of off-site ATMs is likely to grow further.

To address the customer service issues arising out of failed ATM transactions where the customer's account gets debited without actual disbursal of cash, RBI has mandated re-crediting of such failed transactions within 7 working days and mandated compensation for delays beyond the stipulated period. Also, a standardised template has been prescribed for display at all ATM locations to facilitate lodging of complaints by customers.

Use of the ATMs connected through any of the ATM networks in the country became cost free for the customers from April 1, 2009. As on May 31, 2022, the number of ATMs in the country stood at 2,17,853. Additionally, as on May 31, 2022, 8,80,896 micro ATMs have also been deployed by the banks.

10.7 Point-of-Sale (PoS) Terminals and Online Transactions

Point-of-sale commonly known as *checkout* is the location where transaction occurs for the sale of goods or services and customers can pay for their purchases. It is an alternative for an electronic cash register and is referred as PoS terminal, which is nothing but a combination of both the hardware and software used for the checkouts. PoS hardware is equipment for PoS system, which includes card-reading machines, printers, cash registers and computer systems.

Credit card machines are typically connected to the internet, phone line, mobile device or computer to send data to the processor. For most credit card processors, funds are transferred from the customer's bank to the business's merchant account. In some cases, the credit card processor uses a merchant account and holds funds on your behalf, and then directly deposits them into your checking account at your discretion.

What is the difference between a credit/debit card machine and a PoS system? A card machine is simply a card reader and PIN pad whereas a PoS system is a complete checkout terminal that comes with a credit card machine, monitor or tablet, cash register, printer and other peripherals. PoS systems also come with additional software or apps that track inventory, monitor sales, generate discounts, create financial reports, help with marketing and other features.

To facilitate customer convenience, the RBI has also permitted cash withdrawal using debit cards issued by the banks at PoS terminals.

PoS for accepting card payments also include online payment gateways. This facility is used for enabling online payments for goods and services. The online payment are enabled through own payment gateways or third party service providers called intermediaries.

In payment transactions involving intermediaries, these intermediaries act as the initial recipient of payments and distribute the payment to merchants. In such transactions, the customers are exposed to the uncertainty of payment as most merchants treat the payments as final on receipt from the intermediaries.

To safeguard the interests of customers and to ensure that the payments made by them using electronic/online payment modes are duly accounted for by intermediaries receiving such payments, directions were issued in November 2009. Directions require that the funds received from customers for such transactions need to be maintained in an internal account of a bank and the intermediary should not have access to the same. Further, to reduce the risks arising out of the use of credit/debit cards over internet/IVR [technically referred to as card not present (CNP) transactions], RBI mandated that all CNP transactions should be additionally authenticated based on information not available on the card and an online alert should be sent to the cardholders for such transactions.

There were 61,69,175 PoS terminals in the country at end-May 2022, which enable customers to make payments for purchases of goods and services by means of credit/debit cards.

10.8 RuPay

RuPay is an Indian domestic card payment scheme conceived and launched by National Payments Corporation of India (NPCI). It aims to fulfil RBI's vision to offer a domestic, open-loop, multilateral system which will allow all Indian banks and financial institutions in India to participate in electronic payments.

"RuPay", the word itself has a sense of nationality in it. "RuPay" is the coinage of two terms Rupee and payment. The RuPay visual identity is a modern and dynamic unit. The orange and green arrows indicate a nation on the move and a service that matches its pace. The colour blue stands for the feeling of tranquillity which is the people must get while owning a card of the brand 'RuPay'. The bold and unique typeface grants solidity to the whole unit and symbolizes a stable entity.

RuPay was created to fulfil the RBI's desire to have a domestic, open loop, and multilateral system of payments in India. In India, 90 percent of credit card transactions and almost all debit card transactions are domestic. However, the cost of transactions was high due to monopoly of foreign gateways like Visa and MasterCard. In recent years, the usage of credit and debit cards (called plastic money) has increased manifold. It was thought that if this process of transactions is made India-centric, cost can come down drastically. RuPay facilitates electronic payment at all Indian banks and financial institutions, and competes with MasterCard and Visa in India. NPCI maintains ties with Discover Financial to enable the card scheme to gain international acceptance.

RuPay card was launched on March 26, 2012. NPCI entered into a strategic partnership with Discover Financial Services (DFS) for RuPay Card, enabling the acceptance of RuPay Global Cards on Discover's global payment network outside of India.

RuPay cards are accepted at all ATMs across India under National Financial Switch, and under the NPCI's agreement with DFS, RuPay cards are accepted on the international Discover network. All point-of-sale (PoS) terminals in India are under the RuPay platform. To enable this, RuPay has certified major banks in India to accept the RuPay card at their respective PoS terminals located at different merchant locations. In addition to the ATMs and PoS terminals, RuPay cards are accepted online on e-commerce websites.

10.9 Business Correspondents (BCs)

BCs are approved bank agents who provide basic banking services to any bank customer, using a Micro ATM (terminal). BCs and agents play an important role in extending the reach of the banking system to the common man. The business correspondent industry is quite large, with a few lakh agents spread around the country. They are the face of banking to a large part of the population. They are treated as banking outlets and governed by the contracts that they have with the banks. However, they are otherwise unregulated.

The following individuals/entities are eligible to become a business correspondent:

1. Individuals like retired bank employees, retired teachers, retired government employees and ex-servicemen, individual owners of kirana/medical/fair price shops, individual public call office (PCO) operators, agents of small savings schemes of Government of India/insurance companies, individuals who own petrol pumps, authorized functionaries of well-run self-help groups (SHGs) which are linked to banks, any other individual including those operating common service centres (CSCs).
2. NGOs/micro finance institutions (MFIs) set up under Societies/Trust Acts.
3. Co-operative societies registered under Mutually Aided Co-operative Societies Acts/Co-operative Societies Acts of States/Multi-State Cooperative Societies Act;
4. Post offices.
5. Registered companies with large and widespread retail outlets, excluding non-banking financial companies (NBFCs).

Issuer identification number (IIN) identifies the bank with which a customer has mapped his Aadhaar number. IIN is a six-digit number.

10.10 Village Level Entrepreneur (VLE)

VLE is a key stakeholder of the CSC scheme. A VLE is expected to use innovative ways to promote digital financial awareness/access. He may do the following activities:

1. Visit schools and colleges and engage with students to adopt new tools and technologies for financial transactions.
2. Mobilise self-help groups (SHGs) and other voluntary organizations for the purpose.

3. Organise meetings with support of local government agencies.
4. Meeting traders and hawkers to promote cashless transaction practices.
5. Engaging with farmers and householders.

10.11 Working Group on Regulatory Mechanism for Cards

In order to ensure orderly growth of the card segment of consumer credit and protect the interests of banks/non-banking financial companies (NBFCs) and their customers, the RBI constituted a Working Group on Regulatory Mechanism for Cards (Chairman: R. Gandhi). Based of the recommendations of the Working Group, draft guidelines on credit cards were framed by the RBI in June 2005 for all commercial banks/NBFCs with regard to their credit card operations.

The draft guidelines delineated the broad parameters that banks/NBFCs should, at the minimum, take into account with regard to the following:

1. Issue of cards with respect to clear mentioning of most important terms and conditions (MITCs).
2. Interest rates and other charges on customers.
3. Corrective mechanism on account of wrongful billing.
4. Use of direct sale agents and other agents for outsourcing various credit card operations.
5. Protection of customer rights especially in respect of right to privacy, customer confidentiality and fair practices in debt collection.
6. Redressal avenues of customer grievances.
7. Internal control and monitoring systems of the banks/NBFCs for such card operations.

The draft guidelines further stipulated that each bank/NBFC must have a well-documented policy and a *fair practices code* for credit card operations. The *fair practices code* for credit card operations released by the IBA in March 2005 could also be used by banks/NBFCs. The bank/NBFCs code should, at the minimum, however, incorporate the relevant guidelines contained in the draft guidelines released by the RBI.

11

Non-card Electronic Payment Systems

Financial transactions have been seeing high growth over the last few years with multiple avenues for making digital payments.In recent years advancements in banking technology, progress in mobile banking and innovative technologies to facilitate digital payments have enabled large number of small denomination transactions to be handled smoothly in electronic mode. The Government of India has taken policy decisions to encourage cashless/electronic transactions. In its endeavour on moving towards electronic payments, the Central Government has announced a number of incentives. Electronic funds transfer (EFT) system was introduced in the mid-1990s. EFT facilitates transfer of funds from one bank account to another. In the beginning EFT system was permitted only for government transactions and RBI-initiated payments.

11.1 Real Time Gross Settlement (RTGS)

RTGS is a funds transfer systems where transfer of money takes place from one bank to another on a *real time* and on *gross* basis. Settlement in *real time* means payment transaction is not subjected to any waiting period. *Gross settlement* means the transaction is settled on one-to-one basis without bunching or netting with any other transaction. Once processed, payments are final and irrevocable. This was introduced in 2004 and settles all inter-bank payments and customer transactions above ₹ 2 lakh.

The system started operations with four banks and settled only inter-bank transactions. Subsequently, the system was opened for settlement of customer transactions. It was operationalised for settlement of multilateral net settlement batch (MNSB) files from September 2006.

11.1.1 Modus Operandi of RTGS: RTGS system is owned and operated by the Reserve Bank of India (RBI). The system works on a mainframe computer. Members are provided with a participant interface (PI), using which the participants connect to the system at the RBI through the INFINET. The message flow architecture in the RTGS system uses the Y topology. The members communicate through their PI to the inter-bank funds transfer processor (IFTP) which validates all communication and also does the *strip and store* function.

Upon successful completion of a transaction and receipt of confirmation from the RTGS, the IFTP forwards the complete credit information to the beneficiary member's PI. All communication between the PI and IFTP and IFTP to RTGS uses digital signatures (public key infrastructure) to ensure security.

The membership of RTGS is open to all scheduled commercial banks (SCBs), primary dealers (PDs) and others, as may be decided by the RBI. The SCBs are provided with Type A membership, primary dealers Type B and clearing houses Type D membership.

Except Type A members, customer-based transactions cannot be submitted by other members. Type D members are permitted to submit only net settlement batches for settlement under the RTGS system. Other banks and financial institutions can participate as customers of the direct members.

RTGS operations are governed by the RTGS Membership Regulations, 2004 and RTGS (Membership) Business Operating Guidelines, 2004. The members of the system agree to abide by these regulations and guidelines and any subsequent amendments to these documents.

The settlement of RTGS transactions takes place in the books of the RBI. For this purpose, members have to open a 'RTGS Settlement Account' with the RBI at Mumbai. This account is to be funded at the beginning of each RTGS processing day from the member's current account with the RBI, and at the end of the day, the balance in the settlement account is transferred back to the current account of the member.

Members are provided with collateralized intra-day liquidity (IDL) facility to tide over their IDL mis-matches. This facility is provided to Type A and Type B members only. The IDL facility utilised by the members has to necessarily be reversed by them at the end of RTGS day. Failure to do so attracts penal action.

In addition to IDL, the system provides many features for effective liquidity management by the members. These include message release method, queuing management and queue visibility. The Indian RTGS has adopted the FIFO rule for queuing. The system has a centralised queuing arrangement with priorities assigned by the system participant. The participant and system operator can change the priority of messages/revoke the messages in the queue. The system operator would alter the queue only in extreme situations. At the end of the day, all pending unsettled messages are cancelled by the system. The system has a multilateral offsetting algorithm to resolve any gridlock situations that may arise. This process can be configured to be invoked manually or automatically by the system. Since it is mainly a large-value funds transfer system, a floor of ₹ 2 lakh has been prescribed for minimum value of transactions that can be settled through RTGS.

There has been a substantial increase in the volume of transactions settled through RTGS. The inter-bank clearing at all the RBI centres have been migrated to the RTGS system. Further, multilateral net settlements from CCIL, viz. rupee leg of US dollar-Indian rupee settlement, funds leg of government securities settlement and funds leg of CBLO, and the retail net settlement systems operated by National Clearing Cell, Mumbai (MICR cheque clearing, high value clearing, NEFT and ECS) are settled in RTGS as MNSB files. The liquidity management operations of the RBI are also settled through the RTGS system.

11.1.2 Current RTGS Scenario: RTGS system enables transfer of money from one bank account to another on a *real time* and on *gross* basis. RTGS is meant for high-value instantaneous fund transfers. The minimum amount to be remitted through RTGS is ₹ 2 lakh with no upper or maximum ceiling.

The RTGS system was made available 24x7x365 from December 14, 2020.

Only banks, clearing houses and primary dealers can be members of this system, making it a non-level playing field for non-banks. In certain other jurisdictions, non-banks have been allowed access to RTGS.

High-Level Committee on Deepening of Digital Payments (Chairman: Nandan Nilekani) recommended that, "Users must have options to make high value digital payments at any time. The RBI may review the usage patterns of RTGS/NEFT on a quarterly basis and adjust the hours of operation". [1]

There has been a strong push in favour of digital transactions in India, and the costs and charges associated with digital payments have witnessed a steady downswing in the recent past. On June 6, 2019, Reserve Bank of India (RBI) announced waiving off charges on RTGS. The waiver became effective July 1, 2019. The move came on the heels of the RBI-appointed Nandan Nilekani-led committee report for deepening digital payments, which had earlier recommended that banks incentivise digitisation of payments by not charging their customers and small merchants on digital transactions.

11.2 National Electronic Funds Transfer (NEFT)

NEFT is an electronic message-based payment system, and was introduced by the RBI in November 2005 to replace the EFT system [2] which was public key infrastructure (PKI)-enabled and the settlements were effected on a decentralized mode.

NEFT is a nation-wide payments system facilitating one-to-one fund transfer up to ₹ 2 lakh, usually on the same day.

NEFT is more secure, nation-wide retail electronic payment system to facilitate funds transfer by the bank customers, between the networked bank branches in the country. This has facilitated the availability of electronic payment modes at more centres.

The NEFT system is available round the clock throughout the year on all days, i.e. on 24x7x365 basis. NEFT presently operates in batches on half-hourly intervals throughout the day.

In order to popularise the e-payments in the country, the RBI, on its part, waived the service charges to be levied on the member banks, till March 31, 2009, in respect of the real time gross settlement (RTGS) and NEFT transactions. The RBI also provided, free of charge, intra-day liquidity to the banks for the RTGS transactions. With effect from January 1, 2020, banks have been advised to not levy any charges from the savings bank account holders for NEFT funds transfers initiated online.

The service charges to be levied by banks from their customers for RTGS and NEFT were however deregulated and left to the discretion of the individual banks. While some of the banks rationalised their service charges and a few had made it even cost-free to the customers, there were certain banks that had fixed unreasonably high service charges for providing these services to their customers.

In its latest notification dated June 11, 2019, the RBI decided that with effect from July 1, 2019, processing charges and time varying charges levied on banks by RBI for outward transactions undertaken using the RTGS system, as also the processing charges levied by RBI for transactions processed in NEFT system will be waived by the RBI. The RBI also advised the banks to pass on this benefit to customers using RTGS and NEFT with effect from July 1, 2019. It is expected that now even more customers would prefer to transfer funds via NEFT or RTGS as the method is faster compared to offline alternatives such as cheque payments or demand drafts.

11.3 Electronic Clearing Services (ECS)

11.3.1 Background: By the early 1990s, MICR computerised cheque clearing operations at the 4 metropolitan centres, i.e. Mumbai, Calcutta, Chennai and New Delhi had stabilised. However, the volumes in cheque clearing continued to reflect an upward trend, creating considerable pressure on the existing work flow processes. A closer analysis revealed that at par items such as dividend and interest warrants issued by various corporates were contributing significantly to the volumes in clearing. The existing system of paying interest/dividend to the beneficiaries through paper instruments was also fraud prone with frequent reports of postal interception and encashment, often resulting in the real beneficiaries not getting their dues at all, or at other times getting delayed payments.

It was decided that a system needed to be put in place that would: (a) decrease the volumes of paper instruments in MICR clearing and (b) improve customer service by ensuring prompt and secure interest/dividend payments to the beneficiaries. Such a system needed to be cost-effective and serve as an alternate method of effecting bulk, low value, recurring payment transactions, thereby obviating the need to issue and handle paper instruments. ECS scheme provided the answer to these problems.

ECS is a retail payment system which facilitates bulk payments that can be classified as one-to-many and receipts that are many-to-one. The two components of this system are ECS (Credit) and ECS (Debit). This facility is now available at 91 major centres.

11.3.2 ECS (Credit): RBI introduced ECS (Credit) scheme during the 1990s to handle bulk and repetitive payment requirements of corporates and other institutions. It facilitates one-to-many payments such as dividend, salary, interest payments etc. In other words, it facilitates bulk payments whereby the account of the institution remitting the payment is debited and the payments remitted to beneficiaries' accounts. This facility is mostly used for making multiple payments, like payment of dividend to investors, payment of salaries of employees by institutions etc. For this purpose, the company or entity making the payment has to have the bank account details of the individual beneficiaries.

In ECS (Credit), a series of electronic payment instructions are generated to replace paper instruments. The system works on the basis of one single debit transaction triggering a large number of credit entries.

These credits or electronic payment instructions, which possess details of the beneficiary's account number, amount and bank branch, are then communicated to the bank branches through their respective service branches for crediting the accounts of the beneficiaries either through magnetic media duly encrypted or through hard copy.

Corporate bodies and government departments, which have to effect payments to large number of beneficiaries, are the main user institutions. They submit details of payments in magnetic media to the bank managing the clearing house, through a sponsor bank. The user institutions need mandates from beneficiaries, for crediting their accounts under ECS. The corporate bodies also, on their own, advice the beneficiaries about the due date of credit under ECS.

11.3.3 ECS (Debit): This scheme was introduced by RBI to provide a faster method of effecting periodic and repetitive collections of utility companies. It facilitates many-to-one payments such as utility payments and works based on customer's standing mandate. In other words, it facilitates the collection of payments by utility companies.

In this system the account of the customers of the utility company in different banks are debited and the amounts are transferred to the account of the utility company. The company providing this facility has to receive the mandate to collect funds from its customer. On receipt of the mandate, the company advises the consumer's bank to debit the payment due from the account on the due dates.

ECS (Debit) has tremendously minimized the use of paper instruments apart from improving process efficiency and customer satisfaction. There is no limit as to the minimum or maximum amount of payment.

Settlement in this system currently takes place on T+0 basis and the cycle gets completed on T+1 basis. The clearing and settlement transactions through ECS occur at the respective centres. A centralised facility is available at the RBI, Mumbai to receive the ECS (Credit) files meant for credit at the other 14 RBI centres. ECS is operated by RBI and banks.

11.4 Immediate Payment Services (IMPS)

IMPS is a real-time fund transfer platform available 24x7x365. On October 8, 2021, RBI increased the daily limit of IMPS transactions from ₹ 2 lakh to ₹ 5 lakh which should further help in boosting digital payments.

It is a non-card retail payment service operated by National Payments Corporation of India (NPCI) in collaboration with member banks. It is available 24x7. Under IMPS, beneficiary gets funds on a real time basis with the settlement between banks happening on a deferred net basis.

Used mainly for remittances, IMPS has become popular in recent years. Lately, IMPS has been allowed for receiving foreign inward remittances.

11.4.1 Background: Currently, a majority of inter-bank mobile fund transfer transactions are channelised through NEFT mechanism. Under NEFT, the transactions are processed and settled in batches, hence are not real time. Also, the transactions can be done only during the working hours of the RTGS system.

In the above context, NPCI had carried out a pilot on mobile payment system initially with 4 member banks, viz. State Bank of India, Bank of India, Union Bank of India and ICICI Bank in August 2010. Yes Bank, Axis Bank and HDFC Bank joined this pilot in the months of September, October and November 2010 respectively. IMPS public launch happened on November 22, 2010 by Shrimati Shyamala Gopinath, DG RBI at Mumbai and this service is now available to the Indian public. As on May 22, 2022, 647 entities were live members of IMPS which includes small finance banks, public sector banks, private banks, payment banks, RRBs, co-operative banks and PPIs.

IMPS offers an instant, 24x7, inter-bank electronic fund transfer service through mobile phones. IMPS facilitates customers to use mobile instruments as a channel for accessing their bank accounts and put high inter-bank fund transfers in a secured manner with immediate confirmation features. This facility is provided by NPCI through its National Financial Switch (NFS).

The eligible criteria for the banks who can participate in IMPS is that the bank should have approval from RBI for mobile banking service.

11.4.2 Objectives of IMPS: These are as under:

1. Enabling bank customers to use mobile instruments as a channel for accessing their banks accounts and remit funds.
2. Making payment simpler just with the mobile number of the beneficiary.
3. Serving the objective of RBI in electronification of retail payments.
4. Facilitating mobile payment systems already introduced in India with the Reserve Bank of India Mobile Payment Guidelines, 2008, to be inter-operable across banks and mobile operators in a safe and secured manner.
5. Building the foundation for a full range of mobile-based banking services.

11.4.3 Participants:

1. Remitter (sender).
2. Beneficiary (receiver).
3. Banks.
4. National Financial Switch (NFS) of NPCI.

11.4.4 Pre-requisites for Mobile Banking through IMPS:

A. Registration for Remitter:

1. Register mobile number with your bank.
2. Get mobile money identifier (MMID). MMID is a 7-digit number, to be issued by the bank to the customer upon registration. The first four digits are the unique identification number of the bank offering IMPS.
3. Get Mobile Personal Identification Number (M-PIN) from the bank. M-PIN is Mobile Banking PIN—secret password—to be used by customer during transaction for authentication and security.
4. Download software (application) for mobile banking (ensure compatibility of mobile with the application) or use the SMS

facility in your mobile if your bank provides IMPS on SMS.

B. Registration for Beneficiary:

1. Link your mobile number to the account in the respective bank.
2. Get mobile money identifier (MMID) from the bank.

IMPS person-to-person funds transfer requires the remitter customer to make funds transfer using beneficiary mobile number and MMID. Both remitter as well as beneficiary needs to register their mobile number with their respective banks and get MMID, in order to send/receive funds using IMPS. There may be cases where remitter is enabled on mobile banking, but beneficiary mobile number is not registered with the bank account. In such cases, remitter shall not be able to send money to the beneficiary.

11.4.5 How to Send Money?

1. Login to the application and select the IMPS menu from the IMPS. You may also use the SMS facility in your mobile if your bank provides IMPS on SMS.
2. Get beneficiary mobile number and MMID.
3. Enter beneficiary mobile number, beneficiary MMID, amount to be remitted and your MPIN to send.
4. Wait for confirmation SMS for the debit in your account and credit in beneficiary account.
5. You may note the transaction reference number for any future query.
6. Share your mobile number and MMID with the remitter and ask the remitter to send money using your mobile number and MMID.
7. Check the confirmation SMS for credit to your account from the remitter.
8. Note the transaction reference number for any future query.

11.4.6 Benefits of IMPS Fund Transfer Facility:

1. Instant funds transfer.
2. 24x7x365 availability.
3. Credit and debit confirmations to sender and receiver.
4. Simple and easy to use.

5. Fast, inexpensive, safe and secure, accessible.

Transfer of funds through IMPS offers an instant, 24x7, inter-bank electronic fund transfer service from one account to another account through mobile phones. This mode of funds transfer facilitates customers to use mobile instruments as a channel for accessing their bank accounts and put high inter-bank fund transfers in a secured manner with immediate confirmation features.

11.4.7 IMPS Funds Transfer through Internet Banking Channel: Besides mobile phones, IMPS funds transfer can be done through internet banking channels. The authentication is done for the remitting customers as (user ID + internet banking password/transaction password) with appropriate existing two-factor authentication method. As the transaction is initiated on internet platform, the transaction limits of individual banks for internet channel shall apply. IMPS system is used for beneficiary identification and real-time settlement of transactions.

11.4.8 IMPS Funds Transfer through ATM: IMPS funds transfer can be done through ATM, in addition to mobile phones. The authentication will be done for the remitting customers as (card + ATM pin) with appropriate existing two-factor authentication method. Since the transaction would be initiated on ATM, the transaction limits of individual banks for ATM shall apply. IMPS system is used for beneficiary identification and real-time settlement of transactions.

11.4.9 IMPS Person-to-Merchant (P2M) Payments: IMPS P2M service allows customers to make instant, 24x7, inter-bank payments to merchants or enterprises via mobile phone. IMPS provides mobile banking users a facility to make payment to merchants and enterprises, through various access channels such as internet, mobile internet, IVR, SMS, USSD.

A customer can make payment to any kind of merchant using IMPS merchant payments service:

1. Mobile top-up/DTH top-up.
2. Insurance premium payment.
3. Online shopping.

4. Over-the-counter payments.
5. Fees payments to schools/colleges/universities.
6. Utility bill payments.
7. Travel and ticketing.

The key features of IMPS merchant payments service are as follows:

1. Instant inter-bank fund transfer.
2. Merchant needs to get on-board IMPS network with one bank. Customer of any bank in the IMPS merchant network can make payment to merchant through IMPS.
3. Convenient and time-saving.
4. Anytime, anywhere service.
5. Safe and secure.
6. 24x7x365 availability.
7. Instant confirmation to sender and receiver.

11.4.10 Aadhaar-based Remittance Service (ABRS): In ABRS, a remitter can initiate IMPS transaction using the beneficiary's Aadhaar number, which acts as a financial address and which will be linked to the beneficiaries account number. ABRS facilitates in simplifying the IMPS payment initiation process as in this service the customer will have to input only Aadhaar number of the beneficiary for initiating an IMPS transaction. Another important utility of this service will be in disbursal of subsidy payment i.e. electronic benefit transfer (EBT)/direct benefit transfer (DBT) by the Government. ABRS will act as a catalyst in expanding the financial inclusion reach.

11.5 Unified Payments Interface (UPI)

11.5.1 What is UPI? UPI is a system that powers multiple bank accounts into a single mobile application (of any participating bank), merging several banking features, seamless fund routing and merchant payments into one hood.

It is a system for instant electronic payment through user's smart phone. It is an advanced version of immediate payment service (IMPS) which is used to transfer money between bank accounts. Like IMPS, UPI facilitates round-the-clock funds transfer service. It authenticates the identity of the user like a debit card, using the phone as a tool instead of a separate card. It works 24x7 and for 365 days.

One needs a smartphone with UPI application (app) and a bank account.

11.5.2 How to Make Online Transactions through UPI? Following is the 3-step process to make online transactions through UPI.

1. **Registration:**
- Download a UPI app of your bank.
- Register with your account details and create a virtual ID with your name or phone number.
- It is a one time process.
2. **Online Purchase:**
- Add the item to be purchased to your cart.
- Go to payment option and select payment through UPI.
- Provide only your virtual ID to the seller.
3. **Mobile Authentication:**
- You will receive a pop-up window on your phone's UPI app requesting your approval for online purchase.
- Enter the secure pin.
- A confirmation of successful payment will be sent on your phone.

11.5.3 Benefits of UPI: These are as under:
1. It eliminates the need to share user's name, bank account number, IFSC or bank branch.
2. It eliminates the use of physical tools like debit cards.
3. Instant and secure authentication which can be initiated anywhere.
4. It can be used to make online payments of utility bills and school fees.

11.5.4 Virtual Payment Address (VPA): It is an address given to the user of UPI payment system. It is used to transfer funds. VPA replaces the bank account details. It is linked to the bank account address. Since it is not your actual payment address but acts as the payment address (details of bank account), it is called as the virtual payment address.

A. Features of VPA:

1. You can choose it and change it anytime.
2. You can have many virtual payment addresses.
3. No two VPA would be the same.
4. You can link many accounts with one VPA but you have to set an account as the default.

B. Benefits of VPA:

1. You do not give bank account number to receive money.
2. It is easy to remember than the bank account number and IFSC.
3. To be more secure, you can change it whenever you suspect fraud.
4. You can get VPA of your choice.

UPI is currently the single largest retail payment system in the country in terms of volume of transactions, indicating its wide acceptance. One of the initial objectives of UPI was to replace cash for low value transactions. The transaction limit for such transactions which was increased by RBI from ₹1 lakh to ₹ 2 lakh in March 2020 was further increased to ₹ 5 lakh in December 2021.

RBI and the Monetary Authority of Singapore announced a project to link UPI and PayNow, which is targeted for operationalization by July 2022.

Bhutan recently became the first country to adopt UPI standards for its QR code. It is also the second country after Singapore to have BHIM-UPI acceptance at merchant locations.

11.6 Unstructured Supplementary Service Data (USSD)

11.6.1 Meaning of USSD: It is a service which aims to take banking services to every layman in the country. This service allows every customer to access banking services with a single number irrespective of the telecom service provider, make of the mobile handset or the region. The service is offered through a National Unified USSD Platform (NUUP) on a short code *99#. The service can be used for payments up to ₹ 5,000 per day per customer.

11.6.2 Steps to Use USSD Facility: These are as under:

1. Visit your bank branch to link your mobile number to your bank account (can also be done at ATM or online).
2. You will get mobile money identifier (MMID) and mobile personal identification number (MPIN).
3. Dial *99# from your phone.
4. Fill in the first 3 letters of your bank against short name or first 4 letters of IFSC.
5. Choose "Fund-Transfer-MMID" option.
6. Enter the payee's mobile number and MMID.
7. Enter the amount and your MPIN, leave a space and enter the last 4 digits of your account number.

By following the above-mentioned steps, you will be able to transfer your money.

11.6.3 Services Available: Various financial and non-financial services are available.

A. Financial Services: These are as under:

1. User can transfer funds by using MMID and mobile number of the beneficiary.
2. User can transfer fund by inputting IFSC and account number of the beneficiary.

B. Non-financial Services: These are as under:

1. User can check the available balance of the bank account linked to the mobile number.
2. User can generate mini account statement for the bank account linked to the mobile number.
3. User can know the MMID allotted by the bank to the account during mobile banking registration.
4. User can generate/change the M-PIN (mobile PIN) which is like a password and used for authenticating financial transactions.

11.6.4 Benefits of USSD: These are as follows:

1. *99# one number for every Indian to access banking

services.

2. Simple and easy to use.
3. Works on almost all GSM handsets.
4. Works on basic voice connectivity. GPRS connection (internet data plan) not required.
5. Customer need not download any application on the phone.
6. Question and answer driven interaction—simple for everyone to understand.
7. Works even while on the move.
8. More secure than SMS.

In short, the service allows every banking customer to access banking services with a single number across all banks irrespective of the telecom service provider, mobile handset make or the region. A common platform for all banks instead of each bank having to develop a platform is a strategic move by NPCI to help banks and let them focus on customers to enable this service while NPCI manages the technology behind the platform.

11.7 Aadhaar-enabled Payment System (AEPS)

AEPS is a payment service offered by the National Payments Corporation of India (NPCI) to banks, financial institutions using Aadhaar.

AEPS is a bank-led model, which allows online financial inclusion transaction at micro ATM through the business correspondent (BC) of any bank using the Aadhaar authentication. This system is designed to handle both ON-US (intra-bank) and OFF-US (inter-bank) requests seamlessly in an effective way by enabling authentication gateway for all Aadhaar-linked account holders.

It is a payment service empowering a bank customer to use Aadhaar as his identity to access his respective Aadhaar-enabled bank account and perform basic banking transactions. It allows bank-to-bank transaction at PoS (micro ATM). The user has to link his account with his Aadhar number at the bank. User can do as many transactions at any AEPS point without any PIN or password. This service is meant to speed track financial inclusion in the country.

The only inputs required for a customer to do a transaction are as under:

1. Issuer identification number (IIN), i.e. identifying the bank to which the customer is associated.
2. Aadhaar number.
3. Fingerprint captured during their enrolment.

11.7.1 Objectives:

1. To empower a bank customer to use Aadhaar as his/her identity to access his/her respective Aadhaar enabled bank account and perform basic banking transactions like balance enquiry, cash deposit, cash withdrawal, remittances that are intra-bank or inter-bank in nature, through a business correspondent.
2. To sub-serve the goal of Government of India and RBI in furthering financial inclusion.
3. To sub-serve the goal of RBI in electronification of retail payments.
4. To enable banks to route the Aadhaar initiated inter-bank transactions through a central switching and clearing agency.
5. To facilitate DBT [3] of Government entitlements like MGNREGA, social security pension, handicapped old age pension etc. of any Central or State Government bodies, using Aadhaar and authentication thereof as supported by the UIDAI.
6. To facilitate inter-operability across banks in a safe and secured manner.
7. To build the foundation for a full range of Aadhaar-enabled banking services.

11.7.2 Services Offered by AEPS:

1. Balance enquiry.
2. Cash withdrawal.
3. Cash deposit.
4. Aadhaar-to-Aadhaar fund transfer.
5. Gateway authentication service.

11.7.3 Benefits of AEPS: These are as under:

1. Safe and secure and easy to use payment platform by using Aadhaar number and finger prints.
2. Based on the demographic and biometric information of an individual.
3. Eliminates the threat of any fraud and non-genuine activity.
4. Facilitate disbursements of Government entitlements like social security pension, old age pension etc. of any Central or State Government, using Aadhaar authentication.
5. Facilitates inter-operability across banks in a safe and secured manner.
6. No transaction charges.
7. No need to remember bank account number.

Aadhaar is a unique identification number issued by the Unique Identification Authority of India (UIDAI) to residents of India. Any resident of India holding an Aadhaar number and having a bank account may be a part of AEPS. Also, the customer needs to have a bank account for availing AEPS.

Customer should have an Aadhaar number linked with any bank (bank should be a part of AEPS network) where customer has an account. The registration process shall be as per the procedures laid down by the bank providing AEPS service.

A customer may visit a business correspondent (BC) customer access point. The BC using the point of sale (micro ATM) device will be able to process transactions like cash withdrawal, cash deposit, balance enquiry and fund transfer by selecting the transaction of customer's choice. The customer needs to provide his Aadhaar number and his bank name or bank IIN (Issuer Identification Number). IIN identifies the bank with which a customer has mapped his Aadhaar number. IIN is a six digit number.

A point-of-sale (PoS) (micro ATM) device is used to facilitate customers to make cash deposit, cash withdrawal, fund transfer and balance enquiry. The PoS device may be a micro ATM.

11.8 Aadhaar Payment Bridge System (APBS)

It is a unique payment system implemented by National Payments Corporation of India (NPCI), which uses Aadhaar number as a central key for electronically channelizing the Government subsidies and benefits in the Aadhaar-enabled bank accounts (AEBA) of the intended beneficiaries. It is a payment system based on Aadhaar numbers issued by UIDAI and issuer identification number (IIN) issued by NPCI. APBS is used by the Government departments and agencies for the transfer of benefits and subsidies under Direct Benefit Transfer (DBT) scheme launched by Government of India.

The APBS sub-serves the goal of financial inclusion and provides an opportunity to the Government to attempt financial re-engineering of its subsidy management programme. The implementation of APBS has also lead to electronification of a large number of retail payment transactions which were predominantly either in cash or cheque.

APBS eliminates inordinate delays, multiple channels and paperwork involved in the existing system and transfers benefits and subsidies in a seamless and timely manner and directly into the Aadhaar-enabled bank account. In case of change in bank account, customer is not required to convey the bank account details or change in bank details to the Government department or agency. Customer is also not required to open multiple bank accounts for receiving benefits and subsidies of various social welfare schemes. A customer just needs to open one account and seed his/her Aadhaar number in the bank account to start receiving benefits and subsidies directly into his/her Aadhaar-enabled bank account.

11.9 Bharat Interface for Money (BHIM)

BHIM is a national system for account-to-account transfers. It is a one app for all users from all banks. It ensures direct transactions from and to your bank account.

It is a mobile app developed by NPCI based on the unified payment interface (UPI). [4] It was launched by Prime Minister

Narendra Modi in New Delhi on December 30, 2016. Named after Dr. Bhimrao Ambedkar, it is intended to facilitate e-payments directly through banks and as a part of the drive towards cashless transactions in the wake of demonetization of high value currency notes in November 2016.

This UPI app supports all Indian banks which use that platform, which is built over the *immediate payment service* infrastructure and allows the user to instantly transfer money between the bank accounts of any two parties. It can be used on all mobile devices. It has the potential to revolutionize the mobile payments arena. The customers can provide just a registered virtual address for making or receiving payments.

11.10 BHIM Aadhaar (Only for Merchants)

BHIM Aadhaar enables the merchants to accept payments from customers using their Aadhaar number and biometric authentication of transactions.

It is an Aadhaar-based system for merchants facilitating account-to-account transfers. Customers can pay without the need of card/phone. A merchant can accept payment through his mobile phone using a fingerprint scanner.

This mode of payment has the following features:

1. Direct credit transactions from customer's bank account to merchant's bank account.
2. Instantaneous transfer.
3. Authentication by customer's fingerprint and hence highly secure.

Following are the requirements for registration on BHIM Aadhaar:

1. Smart phone with internet facility.
2. Fingerprint scanner attached to smartphone.
3. Aadhaar number seeded to bank account.
4. Merchant on-boarded by his bank.

11.11 e-Rupi

Another digital payment solution launched in August

2021, e-Rupi is a person-specific, and purpose-specific digital voucher where it is not required for the customer to have a bank account and is operable on basic phones, even in areas which lack an internet connection. The first use case of e-Rupi was implemented for Covid-19 vaccination programme which saw more than 2.2 lakh beneficiaries being issued the voucher. On February 10, 2022, RBI increased the cap on e-Rupi vouchers issued by the government from ₹ 10,000 to ₹ 1 lakh per voucher and allowed one voucher to be used multiple times until fully redeemed. This offline payment solution is expected to ensure better digital delivery of benefits of the central and state government schemes to the beneficiaries.

Hence, it is slated to play a major role in strengthening direct benefit transfer (DBT) to citizens at the last mile, making it more transparent.

11.12 Digital Wallet or Electronic Wallet (E-Wallet)

Digital wallet is essentially digital versions of traditional wallet that someone would carry in his pocket. It is a type of electronic card which is used for transactions made online through a computer or a smartphone. The utility of digital wallet is the same as that of a credit or debit card. A digital wallet needs to be linked with the individual's bank account to make payments. This can include purchasing items online from a store. An individual's bank account can also be linked to the digital wallet. He may also have his driving license, health card, loyalty card(s) and other ID documents stored on the phone. The credentials can be passed to a merchant's terminal wirelessly via near field communication (NFC).

Increasingly, digital wallets are being made not just for basic financial transactions but to also authenticate the holder's credentials. For example, a digital wallet could potentially verify the age of the buyer to the store while purchasing alcohol. The system has already gained popularity in Japan, where digital wallets are known as *wallet mobiles*.

11.12.1 Components of Digital Wallet: A digital wallet

has both software and information components.

The software provides security and encryption for the personal information and for the actual transaction. Typically, digital wallets are stored on the client side and are easily self-maintained and fully compatible with most e-commerce websites. A client-side digital wallet requires minimal set-up and is relatively easy to use. Once the software is installed, the user begins by entering all the pertinent information. The digital wallet is now set up. At the purchase or check-out page of an e-commerce site, the digital wallet software has the ability to automatically enter the user information in the online form. A server-side digital wallet, also known as *thin wallet*, is one that an organization creates for and about you and maintains on its servers. Server-side digital wallets are gaining popularity among major retailers due to the security, efficiency, and added utility they provide to the end-user, which increases their satisfaction of their overall purchase.

The information component is basically a database of user-input information. This information consists of your shipping address, billing address, payment methods (including credit card numbers, expiry dates, and security numbers), and other information.

11.12.2 Application of Digital Wallets: Consumers are not required to fill out order forms on each site when they purchase an item because the information has already been stored and is automatically updated and entered into the order fields across merchant sites when using a digital wallet. Consumers also benefit when using digital wallets because their information is encrypted or protected by a private software code; merchants benefit by receiving protection against fraud.

Digital wallets are available to consumers free of charge, and they are fairly easy to obtain. For example, when a consumer makes a purchase at a merchant site that is set up to handle server-side digital wallets, he types his name and payment and shipping information into the merchant's own form. At the end of the purchase, the consumer is asked to sign up for a wallet of his choice by entering a user name and password for future purchases. Users can also acquire wallets at a wallet vendor's site.

Although a wallet is free for consumers, vendors charge merchants for wallets. Some wallet vendors make arrangements for merchants to pay them a percentage of every successful purchase directed through their wallets. In other cases, digital wallet vendors process the transactions between cardholders and participating merchants and charge merchants a flat fee.

11.12.3 Advantages for E-commerce Sites: Quite often, online shoppers abandon their order due to frustration in filling in forms. The digital wallet combats this problem by providing users the option to transfer their information securely and accurately. This simplified approach to completing transactions results in better usability and ultimately more utility for the customer.

Moreover, digital wallets can also increase the security of the transaction since the wallet typically does not pass payment card details to the website. A unique transaction identifier or token is shared instead. Increasingly this approach is a feature of online payment gateways, especially if the payment gateway offers a hosted payment page integration approach.

11.12.4 How to Use Digital Wallet Facility? Digital wallet facility can be used by following steps as under:

1. Download the app on your device.
2. Sign-up by entering the relevant information. The user will receive a password.
3. Load money using debit/credit card.
4. After shopping online, the e-wallet automatically fills in the user's information on the payment form.
5. Once the online payment is made, the user is not required to fill the order form on any other website as the information gets stored in the database and is updated automatically.

11.13 Electronic Toll Collections

National Electronic Toll Collection (NETC) system facilitates an automated and interoperable electronic toll collection structure across the country's network of highways. NETC operates under the brand name Fastag, and it allows tolls to be collected digitally on national highways, allowing smoother movement of vehicles. NETC operates through a linked closed loop wallet, which is funded by the user. Only bank issuers, and acquirers are permitted to operate under NETC.

To sum up, the benefits of electronic payment infrastructure are not yet trickling down to the lower end of the customer segment which still largely uses services like money order and informal channels for transferring money of small value which has much higher cost and time lag for transferring money. There is a need to develop solutions using newer technologies which would allow all segments of the society to gain access to the benefits offered by these facilities.

In order to popularise e-payments in the country, the RBI, on its part, decided to waive off, with effect from July 1, 2019, processing charges and time varying charges levied on banks by RBI for outward transactions undertaken using the RTGS system, as also the processing charges levied by RBI for transactions processed in NEFT system. The RBI also advised the banks to pass on this benefit to customers using RTGS and NEFT with effect from July 1, 2019.

The lack of awareness about new products is not confined only to the members of public at large. It is not uncommon to find that even the branch staff, having direct interface with the banking customers, is not aware of these products and services offered by the bank. This has, therefore, resulted in the continued reliance of the members of public on the traditional methods for availing of various banking services and the benefits of technology have not fully percolated to the level of the customers. There is thus the need to take appropriate measures to increase the awareness of the electronic payment products—not only among the clientele of the banks but also among the own staff of banks so that the members of public can be properly guided and efficient and hassle-free customer service is rendered to them.

Endnotes

1. Reserve Bank of India, *Report of the High-Level Committee on Deepening of Digital Payments* (Chairman: Nandan Nilekani), May 2019, p. 28.
2. Electronic funds transfer (EFT) was a retail funds transfer system introduced in the late 1990s which enabled an account holder of a bank to electronically transfer funds to another account holder with any other participating bank. Available across 15 major centres in the country, this system is no longer available for use by the general public, for whose benefit a feature-rich and more efficient system is now in place, which is the NEFT system.
3. Direct Benefit Transfer (DBT) is a scheme launched by Government of India to transfer the benefits and subsidies of various social welfare schemes like LPG subsidy, MGNREGA payments, old age pension, scholarships etc. directly in the bank account of the beneficiary.
4. Unified payment interface (UPI) of India is a payment system which facilitates the fund transfer between two bank accounts. This payment system works on the mobile platform. Sending money through the UPI app is as easy as sending a message. The customer is not required to give bank account details for the funds transfer through the UPI payment system.

12

Internet Banking

Internet banking facilitates an effective payment and accounting system thereby enhancing the speed of delivery of banking services considerably. However, internet banking has presented regulators and supervisors worldwide with new challenges. Internet, by its very nature, reaches across borders and is, for this reason, engaging the attention of regulatory and supervisory authorities all over the world. In response to the challenges thrown by the internet banking, regulators and supervisors from various countries have prepared their own mechanism of regulation.

12.1 Internet Banking and Electronic Banking (E-banking)

Electronic banking (e-banking) is a generic term encompassing internet banking, telephone banking, mobile banking etc. In other words, it is a process of delivery of banking services and products through electronic channels such as satellite, telephone, internet, cell phone etc. The concept and scope of e-banking is still evolving. Internet banking is a major component of e-banking.

Internet banking offers different online services like balance enquiry, requests for cheque books, recording stop-payment instructions, balance transfer instructions, account opening and other forms of traditional banking services. These are mostly traditional services offered through internet as a new delivery channel. Banks are also offering payment services on behalf of their customers who shop in different e-shops, e-malls etc.

12.2 Distinctive Features of Internet Banking

These are as under:

1. It has removed the traditional geographical barriers as it can reach out to customers of different countries/legal

jurisdiction. This has raised the question of jurisdiction of law/supervisory system to which such transactions should be subjected.

2. It has added a new dimension to different kinds of risks traditionally associated with banking, heightening some of them and throwing new risk control challenges.
3. Security of banking transactions, validity of electronic contracts and customers' privacy etc.—which have all along been concerns of both bankers and supervisors—have assumed different dimensions given that internet is a public domain, not subject to control by any single authority or group of users.
4. It has posed a strategic risk of loss of business to those banks which do not respond in time to this new technology, being the efficient and cost-effective delivery mechanism of banking services.
5. A new form of competition has emerged both from the existing players and new players of the market who are not strictly banks.

12.3 Levels of Banking Services Offered through Internet

Like many other countries, India does not have specific regulatory laws for internet banking. The existing regulatory framework over banks has been extended to Internet banking as well. However, certain guidelines have been issued to banks to recognise the risks arising from electronic modes and to devise control mechanisms that are needed to mitigate such risks. Banks offering internet banking services in India need to comply with the guidelines.

12.3.1 Basic Level Services (or Information Only Systems): These refer to websites of banks which disseminate information on different products and services offered to customers and members of public in general. A bank may receive and reply to queries of customers through e-mail. General purpose information like interest rates, branch locations, product features, loan and deposit calculators are provided on the website of a bank. The sites also allow downloading of application forms. Interactivity is limited to a simple form of e-mail. No identification or authentication of customers is done and there is no interaction between the bank's production system (where current data of accounts are kept and transactions are processed) and the customer.

12.3.2 Simple Transactional Systems: These systems permit clients to furnish their instructions, applications for different services, queries on their account balances etc. However, any fund-based transactions on their accounts are not permitted. In other words, these systems provide customer-specific information in the form of account balances, transaction details, statement of account etc. Largely, the information is *read only*.

Identification and authentication of client takes place using relatively simple techniques such as passwords. Information is fetched from the production system of the bank in either the batch mode or off-line. Hence, the main application system of the bank is not directly accessed.

12.3.3 Fully Transactional Websites: These allow the customers to operate on their accounts for transfer of funds, payment of different bills, subscribing to other products of the bank and to transact purchase and sale of securities etc. These systems provide bi-directional transaction capabilities. The bank allows customers to submit transactions on its systems and these directly update customers' accounts. Therefore, security and control system need to be strongest here.

The above forms of internet banking services are offered by traditional banks as an additional method of serving the customer or by new banks who deliver banking services primarily through internet or other electronic delivery channels as the value-added services. Some of these banks are known as *virtual banks* or *internet-only-banks* (IOBs) and may not have any physical presence in a country despite offering different banking services.

Hence, internet banking, by and large, is traditional banking services delivered through an electronic communication backbone, namely internet. But, in the process it has thrown open issues which have ramifications beyond what a new delivery channel would normally envisage. Therefore, it has compelled regulators world over to take note of this emerging channel.

12.4 Advantages of Internet Banking

The cost of delivery of banking services through Internet is several times less than the traditional delivery methods. This alone is enough reason for banks to flock to internet and to deliver more and more of their services through internet. Not adopting this new technology in time has the risk of banks getting edged out of competition.

In such a scenario, the thrust of regulatory thinking has been to ensure that while the banks remain efficient and cost effective, they must be aware of the risks involved and have proper built-in safeguards, machinery and systems to manage the emerging risks. It is not enough for banks to have systems in place, but the systems must be constantly upgraded to changing and well-tested technologies, which is a much bigger challenge. The other aspect is to provide conducive regulatory environment for orderly growth of such form of banking. Central Banks of many countries have put in place broad regulatory framework for internet banking.

Internet banking has taken roots in India also. A number of banks have set up banking portals allowing their customers to access facilities like obtaining information, querying on their accounts etc. The desire to benefit from the advantages of electronic commerce in financial services has become widespread. Financial services industry is increasingly focused on providing technology-based financial services solutions directly to customers in order to help build and retain customer bases.

12.5 Internet Banking in India

Internet banking—both as a medium of delivery of banking services and as a strategic tool for business development—has gained wide acceptance internationally and is fast catching up in India with more and more banks entering the fray. India can be said to be on the threshold of a major banking revolution with net banking having already been unveiled.

The growth potential of internet banking in India is immense. Further incentives provided by banks would dissuade customers from visiting physical branches, and thus get 'hooked' to the convenience of arm-chair banking. The facility of accessing their accounts from anywhere in the world by using a home computer with internet connection, is particularly fascinating to non-resident Indians and high net worth individuals having multiple bank accounts.

Costs of banking service through the internet form a fraction of costs through conventional methods. The cost-conscious banks in the country have therefore actively considered use of internet as a channel for providing services. Fully computerized banks, with better management of their customer base are in a stronger position to cross-sell their products through this channel.

12.5.1 Products and Services Offered: Indian banks are at different stages of the web-enabled banking transactions. For example, a bank, which is not having a website, allows its customer to communicate with it through an e-mail address and the communication is limited to a small number of branches and offices which have access to this e-mail account. Many commercial banks are still in the first stage of internet banking operations.

With gradual adoption of information technology, the bank puts up a website that provides general information on the banks, its location, services available e.g. loan and deposits products, application forms for downloading and e-mail option for enquiries and feedback. It is largely a marketing or advertising tool. Customers are required to fill in applications on the internet and can later receive loans or other products requested for at their local branch. A few banks provide the customer to enquire into his demat account (securities/shares) holding details, transaction details and status of instructions given by him.

Some of the banks permit customers to interact with them and transact electronically with them. Such services include request for opening of accounts, requisition for cheque books, stop payment of cheques, viewing and printing statements of accounts, movement of funds between accounts within the same bank, querying on status of requests, instructions for opening of letters of credit and bank guarantees etc.

Banks are thus looking to position themselves as one-stop financial shops. Some banks have tied up with computer training companies, computer manufacturers, internet services providers and portals for expanding their internet banking services, and widening their customer base. Setting up of Internet kiosks and permeation through the cable television route to widen customer base are other priority areas in the agendas of the more aggressive players.

Banks providing internet banking services have been entering into agreements with their customers setting out the terms and conditions of the services. The terms and conditions include information on the access through user-id and secret password, minimum balance and charges, authority to the bank for carrying out transactions performed through the service, liability of the user and the bank, disclosure of personal information for statistical analysis and credit scoring also, non-transferability of the facility, notices and termination etc.

The race for market supremacy is compelling banks in India to adopt the latest technology on the internet in a bid to capture new markets and customers. Under mobile banking services, customers can scan their accounts to seek balance and payments status or instruct banks to issue cheques, pay bills or deliver statements of accounts.

Compared to banks abroad, Indian banks offering online services still have a long way to go. For online banking to reach a critical mass, there has to be sufficient number of users and the sufficient infrastructure in place. Though various security options like line encryption, branch connection encryption, firewalls, digital certificates, automatic sign-offs, random pop-ups and disaster recovery sites are in place or are being looked at, there is as yet no certification authority in India offering public key infrastructure which is absolutely necessary for online banking. The customer can only be assured of a secured conduit for its online activities if an authority certifying digital signatures is in place.

The communication bandwidth presently available in India is also not enough to meet the needs of high priority services like online banking and trading. Banks offering online facilities need to have an effective disaster recovery plan along with comprehensive risk management measures. Banks offering online facilities also need to calculate their downtime losses, because even a few minutes of downtime in a week could mean substantial losses.

Some banks even today do not have uninterrupted power supply unit or systems to take care of prolonged power breakdown. Proper encryption of data and effective use of passwords are also mattering that leave a lot to be desired. Systems and processes have to be put in place to ensure that errors do not take place.

Users of internet banking services are required to fill up the application forms online and send a copy of the same by mail or fax to the bank. A contractual agreement is entered into by the customer with the bank for using the internet banking services. In this way, personal data in the applications forms is being held by the bank providing the service. The contract details are often one-sided, with the bank having the absolute discretion to amend or supplement any of the terms at any time. For these reasons, domestic customers for whom other access points such as ATMs, tele-banking, personal contact etc. are available, are often hesitant to use the internet banking services offered by Indian banks.

Internet banking, as an additional delivery channel, may, therefore, be attractive/appealing as a value-added service to domestic customers. Non-resident Indians for whom it is expensive and time consuming to access their bank accounts maintained in India find net banking very convenient and useful.

12.5.2 Information Technology Act, 2000: Government of India enacted The Information Technology Act, 2000, in order to provide legal recognition for transactions carried out by means of electronic data interchange and other means of electronic communication, commonly referred to as *electronic commerce*. The Act came into force with effect from October 17, 2000. The Act has also amended certain provisions of the Indian Penal Code, the Indian Evidence Act, 1872, The Bankers Book of Evidence Act, 1891 and Reserve Bank of India Act 1934 in order to facilitate e-commerce in India. However, this Act does not apply to:

1. A negotiable instrument as defined in Section 13 of the Negotiable Instruments Act, 1881.
2. A power of attorney as defined in Section 1A of the Power of Attorney Act, 1882.
3. A trust as defined in Section 3 of the Indian Trusts Act, 1882.
4. A will as defined in clause (h) of Section 2 of the Indian Succession Act, 1925.
5. Any contract for the sale or conveyance of immovable property or any interest in such property.
6. Any such class of documents or transactions as may be notified by the Central Government in the official Gazette.

Section 72 of the Information Technology Act, 2000 casts an obligation of confidentiality against disclosure of any electronic record, register, correspondence and information, except for certain purposes and violation of this provision is a criminal offence.

In the course of providing internet banking services the banks in India are facing new challenges relating to online opening of accounts, authentication, secrecy of customers accounts, non-repudiation, liability standards and consumer protection etc.

12.6 Internet Banking and the Reserve Bank of India

The RBI has played a proactive role in the implementation of

IT in the banking sector. IT-based initiatives are focused on meeting the three-pronged objective of better house keeping, improved customer service and overall efficiency. The RBI has come out with a Financial Sector Technology Vision Document outlining the approach to be followed for IT implementation for the medium-term period of about three years.

Several initiatives taken by the Government of India as well as the Reserve Bank of India (RBI) have facilitated the development of internet banking in India. As a regulator and supervisor, the RBI has made considerable progress in consolidating the existing payment and settlement systems, and in upgrading technology with a view to establishing an efficient, integrated and secure system functioning in a real time environment, which has further helped the development of internet banking in India. The Government of India enacted the Information Technology Act, 2000 with effect from October 17, 2000, which provides legal recognition to electronic transactions and other means of electronic commerce.

The RBI has been gearing up to upgrading itself as a regulator and supervisor of the technologically dominated financial system. It issued guidelines on Risks and Control in Computer and Telecommunication System in February 1998 to all the banks advising them to evaluate the risks inherent in the systems and put in place adequate control mechanisms to address these risks, which can be broadly put under three heads, *viz.,* IT environment risks, IT operations risks and product risks.

The existing regulatory framework over banks has also been extended to internet banking. These guidelines cover various issues that would fall within the framework of technology, security standards and legal and regulatory issues. Virtual banks, which have no offices and function only online are not permitted to offer electronic banking services in India and that only banks licensed under the Banking Regulation Act and having a physical presence in India are allowed to offer such services. Further, banks are required to report to the RBI every breach or failure of security systems and procedures in internet banking, while the RBI at its discretion may decide to commission special audit/inspection of such banks.

As per guidelines, banks no longer need any prior approval of the Reserve Bank for offering the internet banking services. Nevertheless, banks must have their internet policy and they need to ensure that it is in line with parameters as set by it.

RBI has taken the initiative for facilitating real time funds transfer through the real time gross settlement (RTGS) system. Under the RTGS system, transmission, processing and settlements of the instructions will be done on a continuous basis. Gross settlement in a real time mode eliminates credit and liquidity risks. Any member of the system will be able to access it through only one specified gateway in order to ensure rigorous access control measures at the user level. Further, generic architecture, both domestic and cross border, aimed at providing inter-connectivity across banks has been accepted for implementation by RBI.

With the process of dematerialisation of shares having gained considerable ground in recent years, banks have assumed the role of depository participants. In addition to customers' deposit accounts, they also maintain demat accounts of their clients. Online trading in equities is being allowed by SEBI. This is another area which banks are keen to get into.

Wireless application protocol (WAP) telephony is the merger of mobile telephony with the Internet. It offers two-way connectivity, unlike mobile banking where the customer communicates to a mailbox answering machine. Users may surf their accounts, download items and transact a wider range of options through the cell phone screen. WAP may provide the infrastructure for P2P (person to person) or P2M (person to merchant) payments. It would be ideal for transactions that do not need any cash backup, such as online investments. Use of this cutting-edge technology could well determine which bank obtains the largest market share in electronic banking.

Keeping in view all the above developments, internet

banking is likely to grow at a rapid pace and most banks will enter into this area soon. Rapid strides are already being made in banking technology in India and internet banking is a manifestation of this. A sea change in banking services is on the cards. It would, however, be essential to have in place a proper regulatory, supervisory and legal framework, particularly as regards security of transactions over the internet.

12.6.1 Monetary Policy Implications of Internet Banking: A Central Bank may have its concern about the impact of internet banking on its monetary and credit policies. As long as internet is used only as a medium for delivery of banking services and facilitator of normal payment transactions, perhaps, it may not impact monetary policy. However, when it assumes a stage where private sector initiative produces electronic substitution of money like e-cheque, account-based cards and digital coins, its likely impact on monetary system can not be overlooked. Even countries where internet banking has been quite developed, its impact on monetary policy has not been significant. In India, such concern, for the present is not addressed as the internet banking is still in its formative stage.

12.7 Security and Privacy Risks of Internet Banking

Security risk is a primary concern relating to internet banking. Internet is a public network of computers which facilitates flow of data/information and to which there is unrestricted access. Banks using this medium for financial transactions must, therefore, have proper technology and systems in place to build a secured environment for such transactions. Poor security may create reputational or legal risks for banks, as they may be deemed to have provided inappropriate protection for personal data of customers, with consequential legal and/or reputational damage.

Security in internet banking comprises both the computer and communication security. The aim of computer security is to preserve computing resources against abuse and unauthorized use, and to protect data from accidental and deliberate damage, disclosure and modification. The communication security aims to protect data during the transmission in computer network and distributed system.

12.7.1 Security Risks from External Sources: External threats such as *hacking* [1], *sniffing* [2], *spoofing* [3] and *denial of service* [4] attacks expose banks to new security risks. Open electronic delivery channels create new security issues for banks with respect to confidentiality and integrity of information, non-repudiation of transactions, authentication of users and access control.

When a bank's system is connected to the internet, an attack could originate at any time from anywhere. Some acceptable level of security must be established before business on the internet can be reliably conducted. Following are some familiar forms of attacks:

1. An intruder gains unauthorized access and nothing more.
2. An intruder gains access and destroys, corrupts or otherwise alters data.
3. An intruder gains access and seizes control partly or wholly, perhaps denying access to privileged users.
4. An intruder does not gain access, but instead forges messages from your system.
5. An intruder does not gain access, but instead implements malicious procedures that cause the network to fail, reboot, and hang.

Modern security techniques have made cracking very difficult but not impossible. Further more, if the system is not configured properly or the updated patches are not installed then hackers may crack the system using security hole. A wide range of information regarding security hole and their fixes is freely available on the internet. System administrators should keep themselves updated with this information. Common cracking attacks include the following:

A. E-mail Bombs and List Linking: This is a harassment tool. A traditional e-mail bomb is simply a series of message (perhaps thousands) sent to your mailbox. The attacker's object is to fill the mailbox with junk.

B. Denial-of-service (DoS): DoS attacks can temporarily incapacitate the entire network (or at least those hosts that rely on TCP/IP). DoS attacks strike at the heart of IP implementations. Hence, they can crop up at any platform, a single DoS attack may well work on several target operating systems. Many DoS attacks are well known and well documented. Available fixes must be applied.

C. Sniffer Attack: Sniffers are devices that capture network packets. They are a combination of hardware and software. Sniffers work by placing the network interface into promiscuous mode. Under normal circumstances, all machines on the network can "hear" the traffic passing through, but will only respond to data addressed specifically to it. Nevertheless, if the machine is in promiscuous mode then it can capture all packets and frames on the network. Sniffers can capture passwords and other confidential information. Sniffers are extremely difficult to detect because they are passive programmes. Encrypted session provides a good solution for this. If an attacker sniffs encrypted data, it will be useless to him. However, not all applications have integrated encryption support.

D. Security Hole in the System Software: A hole is any defect in hardware, software or policy that allows attackers to gain unauthorized access to your system. The network tools that can have holes are routers, client and server software, operating systems and firewalls.

Most banks appear to be sensitive to external security threats. Among the issues identified for immediate attention is the development of more robust tools to verify the identity and authenticity of larger value transaction requests. [5] In addition, the banking industry needs to continue to work towards international best practices for encryption requirements, including the legality of electronic signature and records. Moreover, since many banks' internal networks rely on security technology similar to that used to manage their external systems, it is important that bankers also be sensitive to managing the security risk arising from their internal networks. If not managed properly, internal security exposures can also compromise the integrity and confidentiality of bank records and customer data. [6]

Security risk arises on account of unauthorized access to critical information stores of a bank like accounting system, risk management system, portfolio management system etc. A breach of security could result in direct financial loss to the bank. For example, hackers operating via the internet, could access, retrieve and use confidential customer information and also can implant virus. This may result in loss of data, theft of or tampering with customer information, disabling of a significant portion of internal computer system of a bank. This may result in denial of services and extra cost in the form of repairing the damage. Other related risks are loss of reputation, infringing privacy of customers and its legal implications.

Thus, access control is of paramount importance. Controlling access to systems of a bank has become more complex in the Internet environment which is a public domain and attempts at unauthorized access could emanate from any source and from anywhere in the world with or without criminal intent. Attackers could be hackers, unscrupulous vendors, disgruntled employees or even pure thrill seekers. Also, in a networked environment the security is limited to its weakest link. It is therefore, necessary that banks critically assess all interrelated systems and have access control measures in place in each of them.

12.7.2 Security Risks from Internal Sources: In addition to external attacks banks are exposed to security risk from internal sources, chiefly frauds by employees. Employees being familiar with different systems and their weaknesses become potential security threats in a loosely controlled environment. They can manage to acquire the authentication data in order to access the customer accounts causing losses to the bank.

Unless specifically protected, all data/information transfer over the internet can be monitored or read by unauthorized persons. There are programmes such as *sniffers* which can be set up at web servers or other critical locations to collect data like account numbers, passwords, account and credit card numbers. Data privacy and confidentiality issues are relevant even when data is not being transferred over the net. Data residing in web servers or even in internal systems of banks are susceptible to corruption if not properly isolated through firewalls from internet.

Identity of the person making a request for a service or a transaction as a customer is crucial to legal validity of a transaction and is a source of risk to a bank. A computer connected to internet is identified by its IP (internet protocol) address. There are methods available to masquerade one computer as another, commonly known as *IP Spoofing*. Likewise, user identity can be misrepresented. Hence, authentication control is an essential security step in any electronic banking system.

Non-repudiation involves creating a proof of communication between two parties, say the bank and its customer, which neither can deny later. A bank's system must be technologically equipped to handle these aspects which are potential sources of risk.

12.7.3 Physical Security: Though generally overlooked, physical access controls should be strictly enforced. The physical security should cover all the information systems and sites where they are housed both against internal and external threats.

Physical security is a vital part of any security plan and is fundamental to all security efforts. Without physical security, it is difficult, if not impossible, to initiate information security, software security, user access security, and network security. Physical security is achieved predominantly by controlled and restricted physical access to the resources of a system. Physical security involves the protection of building sites and equipment (and all information and software contained therein) from theft, vandalism, natural disaster, manmade catastrophes and accidental damage (e.g. from electrical surges, extreme temperatures and spilled coffee). It requires solid building construction, suitable emergency preparedness, reliable power supplies, adequate climate control, and appropriate protection from intruders. Thus, in broad terms, the focus is on restricting access to the computer area, controlling access to all vulnerable and sensitive areas of the department, and monitoring of all staff and visitors.

Physical access can be secured through the following means:

1. Bolting door locks and combination locks.
2. Electronic door locks.
3. Biometric door locks.
4. Manual logging.
5. Electronic logging.
6. Photo identification badges.
7. Video cameras installed at strategic points.

A bank should also have in place environmental controls to manage exposures to fire, natural disasters, power failure, air-conditioning failure, water damage, bomb threat/attack etc. A few means of obtaining control over environmental exposure are as under:

1. The server room and any other unattended equipment room should have water detectors, smoke detectors and fire extinguishers at strategic points. Use of fire-resistant office materials including furniture should be encouraged. Similarly, electrical wiring should be placed in fire resistant panels and conduits. Furthermore, there should be documented and tested evacuation plans.
2. It is important to educate all stake-holders (users, employees etc.) about the importance of physical security. This education should be carried out as part of social engineering.

Security guidelines, policies and procedures affect the entire organization and as such should have the support and suggestions of end users, executive management, security administration and legal counsel. The top management of the bank must express a commitment to security by manifestly approving and supporting formal security awareness and training. This may require special management level training.

Organizations should make explicit security plan and document it. There should be a separate security officer/group dealing exclusively with information systems security. The information technology division should implement the computer systems while the computer security officer should deal with its security. The information systems auditor should audit the information systems. Logical access controls should be implemented on data, systems, application software, utilities, telecommunication lines, libraries, system software, etc. Logical access control techniques may include user-ids, passwords, smart cards or other biometric technologies.

At the international level, bank supervisors should encourage the development of a comprehensive approach to managing risk associated with both internal and external security exposures. Given the continuing evolution of industry standards, security risk management may be an area where bank supervisors can work collaboratively with the industry to promote the development of sound practices.

Endnotes

1. Hacking refers to the practice of breaking into a computer without authorisation, for malicious reasons, just to prove it can be done, or for other personal reasons.
2. Sniffing involves the use of a software program that is illicitly inserted somewhere on a network to capture ("sniff") user passwords as they pass through the system.
3. Spoofing refers to an attempt to gain access to a system by posing as an authorised user.
4. A denial of service attack represents an attempt to overwhelm a server with requests so that it cannot respond to legitimate traffic.
5. Identification is concerned with positively establishing the identity of the person or organisation conducting the transaction. Passwords are a common approach although evolving approaches such as biometrics may become increasingly prevalent. Authorisation is concerned with establishing the authority that an individual has to conduct a particular transaction.
6. Attacks on internal systems including those by employees are more frequent than external attacks in many organisations.

13

Mobile Banking

Mobile phones, as a medium for providing banking services, have been attaining increased importance. Reserve Bank of India (RBI) brought out a set of operating guidelines on mobile banking for banks in October 2008, according to which only banks which are licensed and supervised in India and have a physical presence in India are permitted to offer mobile banking after obtaining necessary permission from RBI. The guidelines focus on systems for security and inter-bank transfer arrangements through RBI's authorized systems. On the technology front the objective is to enable the development of inter-operable standards so as to facilitate funds transfer from one account to any other account in the same or any other bank on a real time basis irrespective of the mobile network a customer has subscribed to.

13.1 Mobile Banking and Financial Inclusion

Developments in mobile telephony, as also the mobile phone density in the India, present a unique opportunity to leverage the mobile platform to meet the objectives and challenges of financial inclusion. By harnessing the potential of mobile technology, large sections of the un-banked and under-banked society can be empowered to become inclusive through the use of electronic banking services.

The Payment and Settlement Systems (PSS) Act, 2007 empowers the Reserve Bank of India to authorize and regulate entities operating payment systems in the country. RBI has, over a period of time, placed importance on the move towards electronic payments and thereby a *less-cash* society. Towards this end, the RBI has been promoting and nurturing the growth of various modes of electronic payments including the pre-paid payment instruments, card payments, mobile banking etc.

The Payment Systems Vision Document 2012-15 of RBI, reflected the commitment towards provision of safe, efficient, accessible, inclusive, interoperable and authorised payment and settlement systems in the country. Recent experience shows that the share of paper-based instruments in the volume of total non-cash transactions has been declining in favour of electronic payments. Though overall volume of transactions in mobile banking is low, there has been significant growth in the volume recently.

13.2 Mobile Banking: Regulatory Framework

Recognising the potential of mobile as a channel for offering financial services in the country, RBI issued the first set of guidelines on mobile banking in October 2008. The mandate was that all transactions should originate from one bank account and terminate in another bank account. At this time, a few banks had already started offering information-based services like balance enquiry, stop payment instruction of cheques, transactions enquiry, location of the nearest ATM/branch etc. through this medium.

The guidelines issued by RBI in October 2008, permitted banks to facilitate funds transfer from one bank account to another bank account, both for personal remittances and purchase of goods and services. Banks were directed on the regulatory/supervisory issues, registration of customers for mobile banking, to ensure technology standards, interoperability, inter-bank clearing and settlement arrangements for fund transfers, customer grievance and redressal mechanism and transaction limits in an attempt to ensure safe, secure transfer of funds.

Under extant regulatory prescriptions, there is no monetary restriction on fund transfer effected through mobile banking as it is left to the risk perception of each bank and policies approved by their respective Boards.

In line with these guidelines, banks have been offering mobile banking services to their customers through various channels such as SMS, USSD channel, mobile banking application etc. However, real time inter-bank mobile banking payments have been facilitated through the setting up of the inter-bank mobile payment services, now termed as immediate payment services (IMPS), and operated by the National Payments Corporation of India (NPCI) with the approval of RBI. The IMPS has enhanced the efficiency of mobile banking by enabling real time transfer of funds between bank accounts and providing a centralised inter-bank settlement service for mobile banking transactions.

13.3 Various Channels for Mobile Banking

13.3.1 Mobile Banking: SMS-based Channel: SMS is a popular and widely used channel in mobile phones. It is ubiquitously available in all handsets irrespective of make and model and also GSM and CDMA enabled handsets. Most customers are very conversant with the SMS channel and use the same for various services including the short messaging. Many popular mobile VAS services such as cricket, jokes, horoscopes, etc. are based on SMS and used widely by customers.

Given the advantages offered by SMS channel, many banks have offered mobile banking services through the SMS channel. This includes non-financial services such as balance enquiry, mini statement, cheque book request, transaction alerts etc., and financial services such as funds transfer, mobile/DTH recharge, bill payments etc.

13.3.2 Mobile Banking: USSD-based Channel: Unstructured supplementary service data (USSD) is a protocol used by GSM cellular telephones to communicate with the telecom service provider's systems. USSD can be used for WAP browsing, pre-paid call-back service, mobile-money services, location-based content services, menu-based information services, and as part of configuring the phone on the network.

USSD messages are up to 182 alphanumeric characters in length. Unlike short message service (SMS) messages, USSD messages create a real-time connection during a USSD session. The connection remains open, allowing a two-way exchange of a sequence of data. This makes USSD more interactive and advantageous than services that use SMS.

USSD platform which is MNO dependent can be efficiently used by the mobile banking platforms. Realizing the benefits and potential of USSD-based mobile banking, some of the banks have launched USSD-based mobile banking services, e.g. State Bank of India, Canara Bank, ICICI Bank, with the help of telecom aggregators who in turn have tied up with few MNOs. For instance, ICICI Bank has tied up with Idea, Aircel, Tata Docomo, Reliance and MTNL for offering USSD platform to its customers on their GSM network.

13.3.3 Mobile Banking: Application-based: All banks who have received the approval from RBI for mobile banking are offering the application-based mobile banking channel to their customers. Customers can download the mobile banking application and perform variety of services including the following: (a) Non-financial transactions such as balance enquiry, mini statement, cheque book request, (b) financial transactions such as funds transfer, mobile/DTH recharge, bill payments etc

The mobile application is offered on various platforms such as Java, Symbian, Blackberry OS, Windows, Android, Apple iOS etc. Many Banks have made the mobile application available in the app stores such as Google, Apple, Blackberry, etc. for easy search and download by the customers.

Following are the advantages of the application-based mobile banking:

- Applications once downloaded are easy to use for the customers who are proficient in using the smart phone based applications.
- Banks have made these applications compliant with most of the latest operating systems covering the large range of smart phones in use.
- It has been experienced by the banks that once customer has used the application-based mobile banking, he

continues to use the same unless there is a change of the handset and/or mobile number.

- The application-based mobile banking can also communicate using SMS and GPRS (data) channels with the mobile banking system of the bank.

13.4 Challenges Faced by Banks in Providing Mobile Banking Services

Despite the potential for mobile banking and the regulatory provisions enabling greater use of mobiles as a channel for financial services in general, and for financial inclusion in particular, banks are facing some challenges in taking mobile banking to the desired level. These challenges are essentially in two fronts:

1. Customer enrolment related issues.
2. Technical issues.

13.4.1 Customer Enrolment Related Issues: These are as under:

1. Mobile number registration.
2. M-PIN generation process.
3. Concerns relating to security are a factor affecting on-boarding of customers.
4. Bank staff education.
5. Customer education.

A. Mobile Number Registration: For a customer, in order to conduct a mobile payment transaction, his mobile number needs to be registered with the bank. The process for mobile number registration is implemented differently across banks. Currently, the process for mobile number registration involves the following:

- Customer mandatorily needs to go to the bank branch for most of the banks to register his number and fill in the application form (paper-based). After verification, his number gets registered in the CBS and in the bank's mobile banking system.
- Some leading banks have provided the facility for

customer to register mobile number at their bank's ATMs using 2FA authentication of ATM card + ATM PIN.

In both the above cases, the customer needs to physically go to the branch/ATM in order to register his mobile number, which acts as a barrier in many cases, besides delaying the entire process. Further, even where the above process of registration through ATMs is provided, it is restricted to the use of own-bank ATMs and the same is not possible at present by going to any other bank ATMs. The process for mobile number registration needs to be simpler for customer to get on-boarded.

B. M-PIN Generation: M-PIN is the second factor of authentication that customer needs to use in order to conduct mobile banking transaction. Customer needs M-PIN from his respective bank in order to get started with mobile payments. Currently, the process for M-PIN generation is implemented differently across banks, and involves the following:

- For most banks, after the mobile number registration at branch/any bank ATM, customer receives M-PIN via SMS on his registered mobile number. In certain cases, customer receives the M-PIN through postal mail.
- Some leading banks have provided the facility for generating and changing M-PIN from the handset itself using the mobile banking application and providing the authentication parameters as required by the bank (e.g. debit card details such as debit card number, ATM PIN, expiry date). These inputs are captured and sent through registered mobile number, for the purpose of M-PIN generation.
- Some leading banks have also provided the facility to generate and change M-PIN through alternate channels such as IVR, ATM, and internet banking. Customer may be able to make merchant payment using just his mobile number and M-PIN/OTP on the merchant interface. The M-pin can be only interfaced on acquiring bank's interface such as USSD etc. for security reasons. The merchant based interfaces can accept OTP (one-time password) for authentication.

C. Concerns Related to Security: One of the major factors affecting customer on-boarding and usage of mobile banking services is the concern relating to security of transactions effected using the mobile phone. While mobile banking application is an end-to-end encrypted channel, the other access channels (e.g. USSD) are not end-to-end encrypted. However, in order to enjoy the higher level of security available in the application-based mobile banking, the customer's handset has to be GPRS-enabled.

Since SMS facility is available on all handsets, the issue of security can be addressed if the SMS can be encrypted end-to-end, thus allaying any concerns relating to lack of security in this channel.

In addition to this, another important aspect adding to the concerns on the part of customers relate to how their complaints and grievances will be addressed for transacting on this channel—whether through their bank or through their mobile service provider.

D. Bank Staff Training: For effective and efficient implementation of providing mobile banking facilities to the customers it is imperative that the bank staff is well versed and thoroughly trained in various aspects of the mobile banking.

E. Customer Education: Banks must continue to invest in handholding and educating customers to increase the awareness of various aspects of mobile banking. Banks collectively may invest in marketing and advertising for widespread promotion of mobile banking.

13.4.2 Technical Issues: Technical aspects which are posing a challenge relate to the following: (a) access channels for transactions, (b) cumbersome transaction process and (c) co-ordination with MNOs in mobile banking eco-system.

A. Access Channels for Transaction: Once the customer's mobile number is registered and M-PIN is generated, customer may use any of the access channels provided by the bank for conducting mobile banking transactions. Currently, while most banks have provided mobile banking application and SMS facility as access channels, a few banks have also provided other access channels such as USSD etc. Some banks also provide a combination of a few of these channels (application + SMS, application + USSD) for offering better security.

B. Cumbersome Transaction Process: In the present scenario, with various banks offering various channels for their customers to undertake mobile banking transactions, the user experience is certainly not uniform across banks/channels. The customer is required to provide different set of inputs (authentication parameters) for each type of access channel, thus making the entire transaction process cumbersome.

C. Co-ordination with Mobile Network Operators (MNOs): In order to offer a more secure and better user experience to their customers through their mobile banking channels, banks need a greater level of coordination with the telecom service providers.

13.5 Technical Committee on Mobile Banking

Reserve Bank of India constituted a Technical Committee (Chairman: B. Sambamurthy), to study in depth, the present challenges faced in mobile banking, the adoption of particular technologies to meet the requirements of banks as well as vast numbers of mobile users and draw up a road-map for implementation of the solutions. [1]

Major recommendations of the Committee which submitted its report in 2014 were as under:

1. Banks need to explore other means of facilitating customer/user registration process for mobile banking which does not require a visit to the bank branch. The potential of inter-operable ATM networks and business correspondent arrangements has to be effectively harnessed towards meeting this objective. Standardization is required in: (a) user registration for mobile banking, (b) user authentication process and (c) user interfaces. Recognising the crucial role that customer/user awareness plays in adoption of any technology for financial transactions, as well as the need for

optimal utilization of resources, the joint customer education programmes by banks will go a long way in facilitating usage of mobile banking.

2. Mobile network operators (MNOs) need to see a business model in it for themselves and play out their role in ensuring mobile banking reaches its full potential by co-operating with banks in their endeavour to provide the appropriate technology/channel to the targeted users. Mobile banking can result in customer stickiness and reduce churn for MNOs. Mobile banking can increase revenue to MNOs and reduce costs to banks. The current solutions already provided by banks and various technological alternatives available can be put in place through a concerted effort between banks and telecom service providers.
3. Common mobile banking applications and common technological platforms need to be built for reaping the benefits of *network effects*. While bank-specific applications and individual platforms have a major role in building brand loyalty, an alternate uniform and common platform, interoperability and similar seamless transactional experience to the users of all banks would encourage mobile banking.
4. The Government of India can explore the options of offering fiscal incentives/economic subventions to the stakeholders in order to ensure participation of various players to offer the solutions recommended here in this Report. The Committee would like to draw attention to similar law *Lei Do Bem* (Law of the Goods) enacted by Brazil in October 2013 which mandates that smart phones give visibility to Brazilian made apps by either pre-loading phones with these home-grown apps or providing a dedicated market place on smart phones to display them.

Endnote

1. Reserve Bank of India, *Report of the Technical Committee on Mobile Banking*, January 2014.

14

Cyber Space, Cyber Attacks and Need for Cyber Security

Information technology (IT) is one of the critical sectors that rides on and resides in cyber space. It has emerged as one of the most significant growth catalysts for the Indian economy. In addition to fuelling India's economy, this sector is also positively influencing the lives of the people through direct and indirect contribution to the various socio-economic parameters such as employment, standard of living, and health and educational advancement. The sector has played a significant role in transforming India's image to that of a global player in providing world-class technology solutions and IT business services. The government has been a key driver for the adoption of IT-based products and IT-enabled services.

14.1 What is Cyber Space?

Cyber space is a complex environment consisting of interactions among people, software services, devices, networks and worldwide distribution of information and communication technology (ICT).

Owing to the numerous benefits brought about by technological advancements, the cyber space is a common pool used by citizens, businesses, critical information infrastructure, military and governments in a manner that makes it difficult to draw clear boundaries among these different groups. The cyber space is expected to be more complex in the foreseeable future, with many-fold increase in networks and devices connected to it.

One of the biggest attractions of cyber space, as an electronic medium, is its openness and freedom. It is a public domain and there is no restriction on who can use it as long as one adheres to its technical parameters. This has also given rise to concerns over the security of data and information and privacy.

However, cyber space is vulnerable to a wide variety of incidents, whether intentional or accidental, man-made or natural, and the data exchanged in the cyber space can be exploited for nefarious purposes by both nation-states and non-state actors.

The United Nations supports the "promotion, protection and enjoyment of human rights on the internet". The resolution specifically "condemns unequivocally measures to intentionally prevent or disrupt access to or dissemination of information online in violation of international human rights law and calls on all States to refrain from and cease such measures".

14.2 Forms of Cyber Attacks and Threats

Cyber attacks and threats are faced by individuals, businesses and governments. These can take the following forms:

1. **Phishing:** It is the fraudulent practice of sending emails purporting to be from reputable companies in order to induce individuals to reveal personal information, such as passwords and credit card numbers.
2. **Hacking:** Hacking refers to the practice of breaking into a computer without authorisation, for malicious reasons, just to prove it can be done, or for other personal reasons. It is done through bugs and other techniques.
3. **Scamming:** It means creating a fraudulent scheme to dupe innocent people. This has become very common and every day one hears more stories of and people getting duped of massive amounts of money.
4. **Sniffing:** It involves the use of a software program that is illicitly inserted somewhere on a network to capture ("sniff") user passwords as they pass through the system.
5. **Spoofing:** It refers to an attempt to gain access to a system by posing as an authorised user.
6. **Denial of Service Attack:** It represents an attempt to overwhelm a server with requests so that it cannot respond to legitimate traffic. A denial of service attack typically bombards websites with requests, overloading the portal

until its server crashes, thus denying access of the website to legitimate users. Such attacks reduce internet speed to almost zero.

A cyber-related incident of national significance may take any form: an organized cyber attack, an uncontrolled exploit such as computer virus or worms or any malicious software code, a national disaster with significant cyber consequences or other related incidents capable of causing extensive damage to the information infrastructure or key assets.

The only way to protect ourselves from such activities is to be vigilant about our data and protect the data from getting into the hands of scamsters and fraudsters.

14.3 Data Sought by Scamsters

The important data that scamsters look for are as under:

1. Permanent account number (PAN).
2. Passport number.
3. Date of birth.
4. Credit card/debit card number.
5. Card expiry date.
6. PINs and passwords.
7. Bank account numbers.
8. E-mail linked to accounts.
9. Mobile number linked to account.
10. Names of close family members and friends.

No financial institution will call or email customers to collect any of the above data. If anyone is asking for these details, be extra vigilant and do not share this vital information with anyone other than those who can be trusted. Scamsters have innovative ways to gather data and once they gather it, they create innovative scams to dupe people.

14.4 Popular Data Collecting Channels Used by Hackers

The most popular channels used by hackers are as under:

1. **Responding to E-mails:** Responding to e-mails offering jobs and informing about gift delivery, lottery win, tax

refunds etc. can be risky for data protection.

2. **Free Service Websites:** There are many websites which offer free services and their only business is to collect data and sell it.
3. **Phone Calls:** Sharing personal data and vital information on incoming telephone calls.
4. **Free Software Downloads from Internet:** Many scamsters tempt people with free music, movies and games, particularly torrent files which are huge and used for downloading movies. When these files are downloaded, virus also gets downloaded.
5. **Point-of-Sale (PoS):** Unattended receipts, misplaced cards, sharing of PIN.
6. **Public Wi-fi and Devices:** When communication is done through public wi-fi network and device, information can be intercepted or collected.
7. **Social Media Sites:** Scamsters can try to befriend you and collect information.

14.5 Consequences of Cyber Attacks

Cyber attacks that target the infrastructure or underlying economic well-being of a nation-state can effectively reduce available state resources and undermine confidence in their supporting structures.

Large-scale cyber incidents may overwhelm the government, public and private sector resources and services by disrupting functioning of critical information systems. Complications from disruption of such a magnitude may threaten lives, economy and national security.

14.6 Need for Cyber Security

Openness and freedom of use of the cyber space has given rise to concerns over the security of data and information and privacy. These concerns are common to any network including closed user group networks. However, over the internet, the dimensions of risk are larger while the control measures are relatively fewer. The key components of such concern are as under:

1. Authentication, i.e. assurance of identity of the person in a deal.
2. Authorization, i.e. a party doing a transaction is authorized to do so.
3. Privacy or confidentiality of data, information etc. relating to any deal.
4. Data integrity, i.e. assurance that the data has not been altered.
5. Non-repudiation, i.e. a party to the deal cannot deny that it originated the communication or data.

15

Measures to Prevent Cyber Attacks and Threats

Rapid identification, information exchange, investigation and co-ordinated response and remediation can mitigate the damage caused by malicious cyber space activity.

15.1 International Convention on Cyber Crimes

Convention on Cybercrime (also known as the Budapest Convention on Cyber Crimes or simply Budapest Convention), is the first international treaty seeking to address internet and computer crimes (cyber crimes) by harmonizing national laws, improving investigative techniques, and increasing co-operation among nations.

It is the first multilateral legally binding instrument to regulate cyber crimes. As of June 2022, 66 countries had ratified the convention.

This international treaty on crimes committed via the internet and other computer networks, deals particularly with infringements of copyright, computer-related fraud, child pornography, hate crimes, and violations of network security. It also contains a series of powers and procedures such as the search of computer networks and lawful interception.

Its main objective, set out in the preamble, is to pursue a common criminal policy aimed at the protection of society against cyber crimes, especially by adopting appropriate legislation and fostering international co-operation.

The Convention aims principally at the following:

1. Harmonising the domestic criminal substantive law elements of offences and connected provisions in the area of cyber crimes.
2. Providing for domestic criminal procedural law powers

necessary for the investigation and prosecution of such offences as well as other offences committed by means of a computer system or evidence in relation to which is in electronic form.

3. Setting up a fast and effective regime of international cooperation

The following offences are defined by the Convention:

1. Illegal access.
2. Illegal interception.
3. Data interference.
4. System interference.
5. Misuse of devices.
6. Computer-related forgery.
7. Computer-related fraud.
8. Offences related to child pornography.
9. Offences related to copyright and neighbouring rights.

It also sets out such procedural law issues as expedited preservation of stored data, expedited preservation and partial disclosure of traffic data, production order, search and seizure of computer data, real-time collection of traffic data, and interception of content data. In addition, the Convention contains a provision on a specific type of trans-border access to stored computer data which does not require mutual assistance (with consent or where publicly available) and provides for the setting up of a 24x7 network for ensuring speedy assistance among the Signatory Parties.

Further, as conditions and safeguards, the Convention requires the provision for adequate protection of human rights and liberties, including rights arising pursuant to obligations under European Convention on Human Rights, International Covenant on Civil and Political Rights, and other applicable international human rights instruments.

Since it entered into force on July 1, 2004, important countries like Brazil and India have declined to adopt the Convention on the grounds that they did not participate in its drafting. Lately, however, India has been reconsidering its stand on the Convention after a surge in cyber crimes, though concerns about sharing data with foreign agencies remain.

15.2 Efforts of Reserve Bank of India (RBI)

Cyber security is a matter of great concern. Albeit the Government and the Telecom Regulatory Authority of India (TRAI) keep coming up with ways to combat cyber crimes, the number of cyber crimes is growing. The Indian Government is reinforcing systems and establishing a centre for cyber security.

Government has launched schemes such as e-health, e-scholarship for students, e-mandi for farmers, digital lockers, Jeevan Pramaan for pensions, MyGov for citizen engagement etc. Government has taken various steps to minimize cyber security threats in India including training police personnel, judges, and appointing security auditors. Also, the Government has urged big companies such as Facebook, Microsoft, and Google to set up their data centres in India.

Innovations are mixed blessings. They bring benefits as well as pose challenges. Innovations in information technology (IT) are no exception to this rule. The most prominent challenge arising from these innovations relates to the concept of security.

Considering the scope for fraud in the electronic banking area and the possibility of contagion, the RBI—as a regulator and supervisor—has been proactive in addressing the risks associated with electronic banking. The RBI has been promptly addressing issues related to fraud with the use of electronic banking facility. Even after issuing guidelines for a secured electronic banking, the RBI advises the banks, from time to time, on control mechanisms to combat such frauds.

As the banking practices and legislations concerning electronic banking are still in the process of evolution in India and abroad because of technological innovations, there is a need for a constant review of various legislations and regulatory framework relating to banking and commerce. The RBI is monitoring and reviewing the legal and other requirements of electronic banking on a continuous basis to ensure that the e-banking would develop on sound lines and the e-banking related challenges would not pose a threat to financial stability.

15.3 Fraud Management in Electronic Banking

To improve customer confidence in digital payments, it is of utmost importance to keep a control on the number of frauds that occur, and to ensure that customers are not impacted. The RBI has already made rules to limit the liability of customers in the event of fraud. Further, the various banks track fraud in the system, and report it to the RBI. Prima facie, the fraud rates in India appear to be low. Regulation has played a key role in this achievement, and it is felt that the requirements of an additional factor of authentication have helped.

In the context of fraud management, the High-Level Committee on Deepening of Digital Payments maintained, "Managing fraud will require cooperation, and some degree of data sharing across the industry. One solution is to ensure that all fraud incidents, including transaction details are reported to the regulator. This information may be used to create a fraud registry. It is expected that the grievance redressal system will also provide a way for customers to report fraudulent transactions. The resolution must include compensating customers for the fraud that they have suffered, and a report to the fraud registry.

Realtime fraud detection systems could use this registry to rate the risk of fraud for users and transactions.

To better protect users, all users and accounts who are participating in the system must be evaluated for fraud risks (including susceptibility to fraud), and relevant volume, velocity limits be placed on high risk users.

Similarly, all transactions must be rated for fraud risk, and payment schemes may be allowed to reject high risk transactions, or to use additional factors of authentication before processing the payment instructions.

To improve confidence in the system, the RBI must ensure

that once fraud is traced to the source, the culprits are apprehended and prosecuted to the fullest extent of the law. These cases must be publicised to ensure that customers have confidence in the abilities of the bank to prosecute, and that future criminals are deterred". [1]

15.4 System Architecture and Design

Appropriate system architecture and control is an important factor in managing various kinds of operational and security risks. Banks face the risk of wrong choice of technology, improper system design and inadequate control processes. For example, if access to a system is based on an IP address only, any user can gain access by masquerading as a legitimate user by spoofing IP address of a genuine user. Numerous protocols are used for communication across internet. Each protocol is designed for specific types of data transfer.

Choice of appropriate technology is a potential risk banks face. Technology which is outdated, not scalable or not proven could land the bank in investment loss, a vulnerable system and inefficient service with attendant operational and security risks and also risk of loss of business.

Many banks rely on outside service providers to implement, operate and maintain their electronic banking systems. Although this may be necessary when banks do not have the requisite expertise, it adds to the operational risk. The service provider gains access to all critical business information and technical systems of the bank, thus making the system vulnerable. In such a scenario, the choice of vendor, the contractual arrangement for providing the service etc. become critical components of a bank's security. Bank should educate its own staff and over dependencies on these vendors should be avoided as far as possible.

Failure to update a bank's technical system—in keeping with the rapidly changing technology—increases operational risk because it leaves holes in the security system of the bank. Also, staff may fail to understand fully the nature of new technology employed. Thus, education of the staff as well as users plays an important role to avoid operational risk.

15.5 Authentication Techniques

Authentication can be defined as a process of verifying claimed identity of an individual user, machine, software component or any other entity. Thus, an IP Address identifies a computer system on the internet just like a phone number identifies a telephone. The underlying objective is to ensure that unauthorized users do not enter, or to verify the sources from where the data are received. It is necessary because it ensures authorization and accountability. Authorization means control over the activity of user while accountability allows to tracing uniquely the action to a specific user.

Various techniques are available for authentication, password being the most extensively used method. Most of the financial institutions use passwords along with personal identification number (PIN) for authentication. In fact, technologies—such as biometrics, tokens and smart cards—can be used to strengthen the security structure by requiring the user to possess something physical.

15.5.1 Token Technology: It relies on a separate physical device, which is retained by an individual, to verify the user's identity. The token resembles a small hand-held card or calculator and is used to generate passwords. The device is usually synchronized with security software in the host computer such as an internal clock or an identical time-based mathematical algorithm. Tokens are well suited for one-time password generation and access control. A separate PIN is typically required to activate the token.

15.5.2 Smart Cards: These resemble credit cards or other traditional magnetic stripe cards, but contain an embedded computer chip. The chip includes a processor, operating system, and both read only memory (ROM) and random-access memory (RAM). They can be used to generate one-time passwords when prompted by a host computer, or to carry cryptographic keys. A smart card reader is required for their use.

15.5.3 Biometrics: It involves identification and verification of an individual based on some physical characteristic, such as fingerprint analysis, hand geometry, or retina scanning. This technology is advancing rapidly, and offers an alternative means to authenticate a user.

15.6 Firewalls

The connection between internal networks and the outside world must be watched and monitored carefully by a gatekeeper of sorts. Firewalls do this job. Otherwise, there is a risk of exposing the internal network and systems, often leaving them vulnerable and compromising the integrity and privacy of data. Firewalls are a component or set of components that restrict access between a protected network and the outside world (i.e., the internet). They control traffic between outside and inside a network, providing a single entry point where access control and auditing can be imposed. All firewalls examine the pieces or packets of data flowing into and out of a network and determine whether a particular person should be given access inside the network. As a result, unauthorized computers outside the firewall are prevented from directly accessing the computers inside the internal network.

Broadly, there are three types of firewalls.

15.6.1 Packet Filtering Routers: The simplest forms of firewalls are the packet filtering routers which are connected between the host computer of an internal network and the internet gateway. The bastion host transmits message accepted by the router to the appropriate application servers in the protected network. Data of a network is routed through them and they allow only certain types of data into the network by checking the type of data and its source and destination address.

If it is determined by the router that the data is sourced from an internet address which is not on its acceptable or trusted sources list, the connection is simply refused. The main advantage of this type of firewall is that it is simple and cheaper to use and also fast and transparent to the users.

The disadvantage is that if the security of the router were compromised, computers on the internal network would be open to external network for attacks. Also, the filtering rules can be difficult to configure, and a poorly configured firewall could result in security loopholes by unintentionally allowing access to an internal network.

15.6.2 Proxy Servers: Proxy servers' control incoming and outgoing traffic for a network by executing specific proxy programme for each requested connection. If any computer outside the internal network wants to access some application running on a computer inside the internal network, then it would actually communicate with the proxy server, and proxy server in turn will pass the request to the internal computer and get the response which will be given to the recipient (outside user). In other words, there is no direct connection between the internal network and internet.

This approach allows a high level of control and in-depth monitoring using logging and auditing tools. However, since it doubles the amount of processing, this approach may lead to some degradation in performance.

15.6.3 Stateful Inspection Firewall: This type of firewall thoroughly inspects all packets of information at the network level as in the case of proxy servers. Specifications of each packet of data, such as the user and the transportation method, the application used are all queried and verified in the inspection process.

The information collected is maintained so that all future transmissions are inspected and compared to past transmission. If both the "state" of the transmission and the "context" in which it is used deviate from normal patterns, the connection would be refused. This type of firewall is very powerful but performance would also decline due to the intensive inspection and verification performed.

15.7 Cryptography

The process of disguising a message in such a way as to hide its substance is called encryption. An encrypted message is called cipher text. The process of turning a cipher text back into plain text is called decryption. Cryptography is the art and science of keeping messages secure. It uses a *key* for encrypting or decrypting a message. Both the method of encryption and the size of key are important to ensure confidentiality of a message.

There are two types of encryption:

1. Symmetric key encryption.
2. Asymmetric key encryption.

15.7.1 Symmetric Key Encryption: In the symmetric key cryptography scheme, the same key is used to encrypt and decrypt the message. Common symmetric algorithms include One-time pad encryption, Data Encryption Standard (DES), Triple DES, LOKI, Twofish, Blowfish, International Data Encryption Algorithm (IDEA). DES and Triple DES are the commonly used techniques.

15.7.2 Asymmetric Key Cryptography: It is also known as *public key crypto-system.* Here two keys are used. One key is kept secret and therefore it is referred as *private key.* The other key is made widely available to anyone who wants it, and is referred as *public key.* The public key and private key are mathematically related so that information encrypted using the public key can only be decrypted by the corresponding private key and vice-versa. Importantly, it is near to impossible to find out the private key from the public key. Common and more popular public key cryptosystem algorithms are Diffie-Hellman [2], RSA [3], Elliptic Curve etc. In all these, the confidentiality is directly related to the key size. Larger the key size, the longer it takes to break the encrypted message.

A. Public Key Infrastructure (PKI): Public key cryptography can play an important role in providing needed security services including confidentiality, authentication, digital signatures and integrity. Public key cryptography uses two electronic keys: a public key and a private key. The public key can be known by anyone while the private key is kept secret by its owner. As long as there is strong binding between the owner and the owner's public key, the identity of the originator of a message can be traced to the owner of the private key. A public key infrastructure (PKI) provides the means to bind public keys to their owners and helps in the distribution of reliable public keys in large heterogeneous networks. Public keys are bound to their owners by public key certificates. These certificates contain information such as the owner's name and the associated public key and are issued by a reliable certification authority (CA).

PKI consists of the following components:

- **Key Certificate**: An electronic record that binds a public key to the identity of the owner of a public-private key pair and is signed by a trusted entity.
- **Certification Authority (CA):** A trusted entity that issues and revokes public key certificates.
- **Registration Authority (RA)**: An entity that is trusted by the CA to register or vouch for the identity of users to the CA.
- **Certificate Repository:** An electronic site that holds certificates and CRLs. CAs post certificates and CRLs to repositories.
- **Certificate Revocation List (CRL)**: It is a list of certificates that have been revoked. The list is usually signed by the same entity that issued the certificates. Certificates can be revoked for several reasons. For example, a certificate can be revoked if the owner's private key has been lost or if the owner's name has changed.
- **Certificate User:** An entity that uses certificates to know, with certainty, the public key of another entity.

The widespread use of PKI technology to support digital signatures can help increase confidence of electronic transactions. For example, the use of a digital signature allows a seller to prove that goods or services were requested by a buyer and therefore demand payment. The use of a PKI allows parties without prior knowledge of each other to engage in verifiable transactions.

B. PKI and Confidentiality: A PKI could also support confidentiality services using a public-private key pair that is different from the one used for signing. In this case, users need to obtain a separate certificate for the confidentiality public key. To send an encrypted message, a user could obtain the recipient's confidentiality certificate from a certificate repository and verify that it is valid. Then the sender can encrypt the message using the public key. Only the recipient, in possession of the private key, will be able to decrypt the message.

15.8 Digital Signature and Certification

Digital signature authenticates the identity of a sender, through the private, cryptographic key. In addition, every digital signature is different because it is derived from the content of the message itself. The combination of identity authentication and singularly unique signatures results in a transmission that can not be repudiated.

Digital signature can be applied to any data transmission, including e-mail. To generate digital signature, the original, unencrypted message is processed through mathematical algorithms that generate a *message digest* (a unique character representation of data). This process is known as *hashing*. The message digest is then encrypted with the private key and sent along with the message which can also be encrypted. The recipient receives both the message and encrypted message digest. The recipient decrypts the message digest using the sender's public key, and then runs the message through the hash function again. If the resulting message digest matches the one sent with the message, the message has not been altered and data integrity is verified. Because the message digest was encrypted using the private key, the sender can be identified and bound to the specific message.

15.8.1 Certification Authorities and Digital Certificates: Certificate authorities and digital certificates are emerging to further address the issues of authentication, non-repudiation, data privacy and cryptographic key management.

A certificate authority (CA) is a trusted third party that verifies the identity of a party to a transaction. To do this, the CA vouches for the identity of a party by attaching the CA's digital signature to any messages, public keys, etc., which are transmitted. The CA must be trusted by the parties involved, and identities must have been proven to the CA beforehand.

Digital certificates are messages that are signed with the CA's private key. They identify the CA, the represented party, and even include the represented party's public key.

15.8.2 Secure Socket Layer (SSL): SSL is designed to make use of TCP to provide a reliable end-to-end secure service. The SSL servers have digital certificates issued by certifying authorities so that the clients can authenticate the service provider, e.g. a bank. The servers use a password/PIN/digital certificate to authenticate clients. Once the clients and server have authenticated each other, they establish a session key for encryption of messages.

15.9 Tools

Tools are extremely useful in monitoring and controlling networks, systems and users. Some of the system administration and network management tools are as follows:

15.9.1 Scanners: Scanners are programmes that automatically detect security weaknesses in remote or local hosts. Scanners query the TCP/IP port and record the target's response and can reveal the information like services that are currently running, users owning those services, whether anonymous logins are supported, and whether certain network services require authentication. Scanners are important because they reveal weaknesses in the network. There are many security vulnerabilities on any given platform. Scanners can do an excellent security audit and then system can be suitably upgraded.

System administrators may use scanners to find out weaknesses in their system and take preventive measures. Scanners can be used to gather preliminary data for an audit. Scanners offer a quick overview of TCP/IP security.

15.9.2 Sniffers: Sniffers are devices that capture network packets. They analyze network traffic and identify potential areas of concern. For example, if one segment of the network is performing poorly or packet delivery seems incredibly slow or machines inexplicably lock up on a network boot, then sniffers can determine the precise cause. Sniffers are always a combination of hardware and software components. Proprietary sniffers are generally expensive (vendors often package them on special computers that are *optimized* for sniffing).

15.9.3 Intrusion Detection Tools: An intrusion attempt or a threat is defined as the potential possibility of a deliberate unauthorized attempt to access or manipulate information or render a system unreliable or unusable. Different approaches are used to detect these intrusion attempts. Some intrusion detection systems (IDS) are based on audit logs provided by the operating system, i.e. detecting attacks by watching for suspicious patterns of activity on a single computer system. This type of IDS called host-based IDS is good at discerning attacks that are initiated by local users which involve misuse of the capabilities of one system. The host-based IDS can interpret only high-level logging information and they cannot detect low-level network events such as denial-of-service attacks. The network-based approach can be effectively used to detect these low level denial-of-service attacks. Distributed intrusion detection systems (DIDS) take data from various hosts, network components and network monitors and try to detect intrusions from the collected data.

15.9.4 Network-based Intrusion Detection Systems (NIDS): These are based on interpretation of raw network traffic. They attempt to detect attacks by watching patterns of suspicious activity in this traffic. NIDS are good at discerning attacks that involve low-level manipulation of the network, and can easily correlate attacks against multiple machines on a network. An intrusion detection system detects the attacks in real-time and informs system administrator about it to take appropriate action. As a result, exposure to the intrusion and the possible damage caused to the data or systems can be countered.

The penetration testing may also be carried out by engaging outside experts often called *ethical hackers*.

Electronic banking is making rapid strides worldwide due to evolving communication technology. Penetration of internet banking is increasing in most countries. Wireless application protocol (WAP) is an emerging service which banks worldwide are also offering. The stiff competition in this area exposes banks to substantial risks. While existing regulations and legislations applicable to traditional banking are being extended to internet banking, it is recognized that internet security, customer authentication and other issues such as technology outsourcing pose unique risks.

World over, the Central Banks are addressing such issues with focused attention. Special legislations and regulations are being framed by the regulators and supervisors for proper management of the different types of risks posed by these services. The reliance on outsourcing is an area where regulators and supervisors are focusing their attention, with banks having to regularly review and test business continuity, recovery and incidence response plans in order to maintain their reputation of trust.

Consumer protection and data privacy are areas which assume great significance when banking transactions are carried over a medium as insecure as the internet. Many countries are looking at special consumer protection/data privacy legislation for an e-commerce environment.

The presence of *virtual banks* or *internet-only-banks* and the licensing requirements required for such entities are also areas which are being looked into by authorities. Another concern among the regulators and supervisors is to meet the challenges of *virtual* cross-border banking, particularly in the light of the possibility of increased money laundering activities through the medium of internet. Internet banking is universally seen as a welcome development and efforts are being made to put in place systems to manage and control the risks involved without restricting this service.

15.10 Digital Forensics

Digital forensic is a branch of forensic science encompassing the recovery and investigation of material found in digital devices, often in relation to computer crime. The term digital forensics was originally used as a synonym for computer forensics but has expanded to cover investigation of all devices capable of storing digital data. With roots in the personal computing revolution of the late 1970s and early 1980s, the discipline evolved in a haphazard manner during the 1990s, and it was not until the early 21st century that national policies emerged.

Digital forensics investigations have a variety of applications. The most common is to support or refute a hypothesis before criminal or civil courts. Criminal cases involve the alleged breaking of laws that are defined by legislation and that are enforced by the police and prosecuted by the state, such as murder, theft and assault against the person. Civil cases on the other hand deal with protecting the rights and property of individuals (often associated with family disputes) but may also be concerned with contractual disputes between commercial entities where a form of digital forensics referred to as electronic discovery (e-discovery) may be involved. Forensics may also feature in the private sector; such as during internal corporate investigations or intrusion investigation.

The technical aspect of an investigation is divided into several sub-branches, relating to the type of digital devices involved: computer forensics, network forensics, forensic data analysis and mobile device forensics. The typical forensic process encompasses the seizure, forensic imaging (acquisition) and analysis of digital media and the production of a report into collected evidence.

As well as identifying direct evidence of a crime, digital forensics can be used to attribute evidence to specific suspects, confirm alibis or statements, determine intent, identify sources, or authenticate documents. Investigations are much broader in scope than other areas of forensic analysis (where the usual aim is to provide answers to a series of simpler questions) often involving complex time-lines or hypotheses.

Digital forensics is commonly used in both criminal law and private investigation. Traditionally it has been associated with criminal law, where evidence is collected to support or oppose a hypothesis before the courts. As with other areas of forensics this is often a part of a wider investigation spanning a number of disciplines. In some cases, the collected evidence is used as a form of intelligence gathering, used for other purposes than court proceedings (for example to locate, identify or halt other crimes). As a result, intelligence gathering is sometimes held to a less strict forensic standard.

In civil litigation or corporate matters digital forensics forms part of the electronic discovery (or e-discovery) process. Forensic procedures are similar to those used in criminal investigations, often with different legal requirements and limitations. Outside of the courts digital forensics can form a part of internal corporate investigations.

A specialist forensic examination into the nature and extent of the attack is performed as a damage limitation exercise, both to establish the extent of any intrusion and in an attempt to identify the attacker. Such attacks were commonly conducted over phone lines during the 1980s, but in the modern era are usually propagated over the Internet.

The main focus of digital forensics investigations is to recover objective evidence of a criminal activity (termed actus reus in legal parlance). However, the diverse range of data held in digital devices can help with other areas of inquiry.

Digital forensics investigation is not restricted to retrieve data merely from the computer, as laws are breached by the criminals and small digital devices (e.g. tablets, smart phones, flash drives) are now extensively used. Some of these devices have volatile memory while some have non-volatile memory. Sufficient methodologies are available to retrieve data from volatile memory. However, there is lack of detailed methodology or a framework for data retrieval from non-volatile memory sources. Depending on the type of devices, media or artefacts, digital forensics investigation is branched into various types.

15.11 Cyber Security Audit

Cyber security audits are a valuable tool for organisations that have not yet documented their internal and external risks, vulnerabilities and threat exposure. It is also applicable to businesses that have expanded, implementing various software and security controls but are inevitably overwhelmed by the volume of data being processed in daily communications.

A cyber security audit is designed to be a comprehensive review and analysis of business IT infrastructure. A cyber security audit helps to mitigate the consequences of a breach and demonstrate that the organisation has taken the necessary steps to protect client and company data.

A cyber security audit is designed to be a comprehensive review and analysis of IT infrastructure of a business. It identifies threats and vulnerabilities, exposing weaknesses and high-risk practices.

Regulations such as the GDPR (General Data Protection Regulation) can impose hefty penalties in the event of a breach that results in exploited data.

The audit itself is divided into two distinct phases, a gap analysis and a vulnerability assessment. The vulnerability assessment service assists in preventing network attacks by identifying the vulnerabilities and configuration issues that hackers use to penetrate your network.

15.12 Artificial Intelligence (AI)

AI or machine learning (ML) is a technology or a computer language that focuses on making intelligent machines that can assist and automate processes. AI services train the software to think like a human brain, with the help of algorithms used under machine learning development services.

The primary mission of machine learning is to work on programming algorithms that give a capability to machines by receiving information and statistically analyzing data to providing acceptable outputs. AI and ML in data security could be technologies and algorithms that can help organizations in achieving their goal of safeguarding their information.

AI and ML are technologies that are used by IBM Watson and are helping other organizations in improving data security and cyber attacks. The technologies algorithm focuses on detecting threats and loopholes in the earlier stages of attack implementation. IBM QRadar, an advisor powered by Watson, assists businesses in finding the cyber attacks and safeguards the data of organizations.

The role of artificial intelligence in the industry is crucial as the world is smarter and more connected than ever before.

For more details, see chapter 3 of this book.

Endnotes

1. Reserve Bank of India, *Report of the High-Level Committee on Deepening of Digital Payments* (Chairman: Nandan Nilekani), May 2019, p. 104.
2. Diffie-Hellman: This is the first public key algorithm invented. It gets its security from the difficulty of calculating discrete logarithms in a finite field. Diffie-Hellman method can be used for distribution of keys to be used for symmetric encryption.
3. RSA: Named after its three inventors, Ron Rivest, Adi Shamir and Leonard Adleman, who first introduced the algorithm in 1978, RSA gets its security from the difficulty of factoring large numbers. The public and private keys are function of a pair of large (100 or 200 digits or even larger) prime numbers. The pair is used for asymmetric encryption.

16

National Cyber Security Policy (NCSP)

India had no cyber security policy before 2013. Government unveiled a National Cyber Security Policy on July 2, 2013.

NCSP, 2013 is a policy framework by Government of India. It aims at protecting the public and private infrastructure from cyber attacks. The policy also intends to safeguard "information, such as personal information (of web users), financial and banking information and sovereign data". It defines cyber space as a complex environment consisting of interactions between people, software services supported by worldwide distribution of information and communication technology.

Vision: To build a secure and resilient cyberspace for citizens, business and government.

Mission: To protect information and information infrastructure in cyberspace, build capabilities to prevent and respond to cyber threat, reduce vulnerabilities and minimize damage from cyber incidents through a combination of institutional structures, people, processes, technology and cooperation.

16.1 Objectives of NCSP

Objectives of NCSP are as under:

1. To create a secure cyber ecosystem in the country, generate adequate trust and confidence in IT system and transactions in cyberspace and thereby enhance adoption of IT in all sectors of the economy.
2. To create an assurance framework for design of security policies and promotion and enabling actions for compliance to global security standards and best practices by way of conformity assessment (product, process, technology and people).

3. To strengthen the regulatory framework for ensuring a secure cyberspace ecosystem.
4. To enhance and create national and sectoral level 24x7 mechanism for obtaining strategic information regarding threats to ICT infrastructure, creating scenarios for response, resolution and crisis management through effective predictive, preventive, protective response and recovery actions.
5. To enhance the protection and resilience of nation's critical information infrastructure by operating a 24x7 National Critical Information Infrastructure Protection Centre (NCIIPC) and mandating security practices related to the design, acquisition, development, use and operation of information resources.
6. To develop suitable indigenous security technologies through frontier technology research, solution-oriented research, proof of concept, pilot development, transition, diffusion and commercialization leading to widespread deployment of secure ICT products/processes in general and specifically for addressing national security requirements.
7. To improve visibility of integrity of ICT products and services by establishing infrastructure for testing and validation of security of such product.
8. To create workforce for 5,00,000 professionals skilled in next 5 years through capacity building, skill development and training.
9. To provide fiscal benefit to businesses for adoption of standard security practices and processes.
10. To enable Protection of information while in process, handling, storage and transit so as to safeguard privacy of citizen's data and reducing economic losses due to cyber crime or data theft.
11. To enable effective prevention, investigation and prosecution of cyber crime and enhancement of law enforcement capabilities through appropriate legislative intervention.

12. To create a culture of cyber security and privacy enabling responsible user behaviour and actions through an effective communication and promotion strategy.
13. To develop effective public-private-partnerships and collaborative engagements through technical and operational co-operation and contribution for enhancing the security of cyber space.
14. To enhance global co-operation by promoting shared understanding and leveraging relationships for furthering the cause of security of cyber space.

16.2 Strategies of NCSP

1. Creating a secure cyber ecosystem.
2. Creating an assurance framework.
3. Encouraging open standards.
4. Strengthening the regulatory framework.
5. Creating mechanism for security threat early warning, vulnerability management and response to security threats.
6. Securing e-governance services.
7. Protection and resilience of critical information infrastructure.
8. Promotion of research and development in cyber security.
9. Reducing supply chain risks
10. Human resources development.
11. Creating cyber security awareness.
12. Developing effective public-private-partnership (PPP).
13. Information sharing and co-operation.
14. Prioritized approach for implementation.

16.2.1 Creating a Secure Cyber Ecosystem:

1. To designate a national nodal agency to co-ordinate all matters related to cyber security in the country, with clearly defined roles and responsibilities.
2. To encourage all organizations, private and public to designate a member of senior management as chief information security officer (CISO), responsible for cyber security efforts and initiatives.

3. To encourage all organizations to develop information security policies duly integrated with their business plans and implement such policies as per international best practices. Such policies should include establishing standards and mechanisms for secure information flow, crisis management plan, proactive security posture assessment and forensically-enabled information infrastructure.
4. To ensure that all organizations earmark a specific budget for implementing cyber security initiatives and for meeting emergency response arising out of cyber incidents.
5. To provide fiscal schemes and incentives to encourage entities to install, strengthen and upgrade information infrastructure with respect to cyber security.
6. To prevent occurrence and recurrence of cyber incidents by way of incentives for technology development, cyber security compliance and proactive actions.
7. To establish a mechanism for sharing information and for identifying and responding to cyber security incidents and for co-operation in restoration efforts.
8. To encourage entities to adopt guidelines for procurement of trustworthy ICT products and provide for procurement of indigenously manufactured ICT products that have security implications.

16.2.2 Creating an Assurance Framework:

1. To promote adoption of global best practices in information security and compliance and thereby enhance cyber security posture.
2. To create infrastructure for conformity assessment and certification of compliance to cyber security best practices, and standards and guidelines.
3. To enable implementation of global security best practices in formal risk assessment and risk management processes, business continuity management and cyber crisis management plan by all entities within Government and in critical sectors, to reduce the risk of disruption and improve the security posture.

4. To identify and classify information infrastructure facilities and assets at entity level with respect to risk perception for undertaking commensurate security protection measures.
5. To encourage secure application/software development processes based on global best practices.
6. To create conformity assessment framework for periodic verification of compliance to best practices, standards and guidelines on cyber security.
7. To encourage all entities to periodically test and evaluate the adequacy and effectiveness of technical and operational security control measures implemented in IT systems and in networks.

16.2.3 Encouraging Open Standards:

1. To encourage use of open standards to facilitate interoperability and data exchange among different products and services.
2. To promote a consortium of Government and private sector to enhance the availability of tested and certified IT products based on open standards.

11.2.4 Strengthening the Regulatory Framework:

1. To develop a dynamic legal framework and its periodic review to address the cyber security challenges arising out of technological developments in cyber space and its harmonization with international frameworks including those related to internet governance.
2. To mandate periodic audit and evaluation of the adequacy and effectiveness of security of information infrastructure as may be appropriate, with respect to regulatory framework.
3. To enable, educate and facilitate awareness of the regulatory framework.

16.2.5 Creating Mechanism for Security Threat Early Warning, Vulnerability Management and Response to Security Threats:

1. To create national level systems, processes, structures and mechanisms to generate necessary situational scenario of existing and potential cyber security threats and enable

timely information sharing for proactive, preventing and protective actions by individual entities.

2. To operate a 24x7 National Level Computer Emergency Response Team (CERT) to function as a nodal agency for co-ordination of all efforts for cyber security emergency response and crisis management.
3. To operationalize 24x7 sectoral CERTs for all co-ordination and communication actions within the respective sectors for effective incidence response and resolution and cyber crisis management.
4. To implement Cyber Crisis Management Plan for dealing with cyber related incidents impacting critical national processes or endangering public safety and security of the nation, by way of well co-ordinated multi-disciplinary approach at the national sectoral as well as entity levels.
5. To conduct and facilitate regular cyber security drills at national, sectoral and entity levels to enable assessment of security posture and level of emergency preparedness in resisting and dealing with cyber security incidents.

16.2.6 Securing E-governance Services:

1. To mandate implementation of global security best practices, business continuity management and cyber crisis management plan for all e-governance initiatives in the country, to reduce the risk of disruption and improve the security posture.
2. To encourage wider usage of public key infrastructure (PKI) within government for trusted communication and transactions.
3. To engage information security professionals and organizations to assist e-governance initiatives and ensure conformance to security best practices.

16.2.7 Protection and Resilience of Critical Information Infrastructure:

1. To develop a plan for protection of critical information infrastructure and its integration with business plan at the entity level and implement such plan. The plans shall

include establishing mechanisms for secure information flow, guidelines and standards, crisis management plan, proactive security posture assessment and forensically-enabled information infrastructure.

2. To operate a 24x7 National Critical Information Infrastructure Protection Centre (NCIIPC) to function as the nodal agency for critical information infrastructure protection in the country.
3. To facilitate identification, prioritisation, assessment, remediation and protection of critical infrastructure and key resources based on the plan for protection of critical information infrastructure.
4. To mandate implementation of global security best practices, business continuity management and cyber crisis management plan by all critical sector entities, to reduce the risk of disruption and improve the security posture.
5. To encourage and mandate as appropriate, the use of validated and certified IT products.
6. To mandate security audit of critical information infrastructure on a periodic basis.
7. To mandate certification for all security roles to those involved in operation of critical information infrastructure.
8. To mandate secure application/software development process based on global best practices.

16.2.8 Promotion of Research and Development in Cyber Security:

1. To undertake research and development programmes for addressing all aspects of development aimed at short-term, medium-term and long-term goals which include development of trustworthy systems, their testing, deployment and maintenance throughout the life cycle.
2. To encourage research and development to produce cost-effective, tailor-made indigenous security solutions meeting a wider range of cyber security challenges and target for export markets.
3. To facilitate transition, diffusion and commercialization of

the outputs of research and development into commercial products and services for use in public and private sectors.

4. To set up centres of excellence in areas of strategic importance for the point of security of cyber space.
5. To collaborate in joint research and development projects with industry and academia in frontline technologies and solution-oriented research.

16.2.9 Reducing Supply Chain Risks:

1. To create and maintain testing infrastructure and facilities for IT security product evaluation and compliance verification as per global standards and practices.
2. To build trusted relationships with product/system vendors and service providers for improving end-to-end supply chain security visibility.
3. To create awareness of the threats, vulnerabilities and consequences of breach of security among entities for managing supply chain risks related to IT (products, systems or services) procurement.

16.2.10 Human Resources Development:

1. To foster education and training programmes both in formal and informal sectors to support the nation's cyber security needs and build capacity.
2. To establish cyber security training infrastructure across the country by way of public-private-partnership arrangements.
3. To establish cyber security concept labs for awareness and skill development in key areas.
4. To establish institutional mechanisms for capacity building for law enforcement agencies.

16.2.11 Creating Cyber Security Awareness:

1. To promote and launch a comprehensive national awareness programme on security of cyber space.
2. To sustain security literacy awareness and publicity campaign through electronic media to help citizens to be aware of the challenges of cyber security.
3. To conduct, support and enable cyber security workshops/seminars and certifications.

16.2.12 Developing Effective Public-Private-Partnership (PPP):

1. To facilitate collaboration and co-operation among stakeholder entities including private sector, in the area of cyber security in general and protection of critical information infrastructure in particular for actions related to cyber threats, vulnerabilities, breaches, potential protective measures, and adoption of best practices.
2. To create models for collaborations and engagements with all relevant stakeholders.
3. To create a think tank for cyber security policy inputs, discussion and deliberations.

16.2.13 Information Sharing and Co-operation:

1. To develop bilateral and multilateral relationships in the area of cyber security with other countries.
2. To enhance national and global co-operation among security agencies, defence agencies and forces, law enforcement agencies and judicial systems.
3. To create mechanisms for dialogue related to technical and operational aspects with industry in order to facilitate efforts in recovery and resilience of systems including critical information infrastructure.

16.2.14 Prioritized Approach for Implementation:

1. To adopt a prioritized approach to implement the policy so as to address the most critical areas in the first instance.

17

Data Protection Strategies and Technologies

17.1 What is Data Protection?

Data protection is the process of safeguarding important information from corruption, compromise or loss.

The importance of data protection increases as the amount of data created and stored continues to grow at unprecedented rates. There is also little tolerance for downtime that can make it impossible to access important information.

Consequently, a large part of a data protection strategy is ensuring that data can be restored quickly after any corruption or loss. Protecting data from compromise and ensuring data privacy are other key components of data protection.

The key principles of data protection are to safeguard and make available data under all circumstances. The term *data protection* is used to describe both the operational backup of data and business continuity/disaster recovery (BC/DR).

17.2 Data Protection Strategies

Data protection strategies are evolving along two lines:

1. Data availability.
2. Data management.

17.2.1 Data Availability: It ensures users have the data they need to conduct business even if the data is damaged or lost.

17.2.2 Data Management: There are two key areas of data management used in data protection: (a) data lifecycle management and (b) information lifecycle management.

Data lifecycle management is the process of automating the movement of critical data to online and offline storage. Information lifecycle management is a comprehensive strategy for valuing, cataloguing and protecting information assets from application and user errors, malware and virus attacks, machine failure or facility outages and disruptions.

More recently, data management has come to include finding ways to unlock business value from otherwise dormant copies of data for reporting, analytics and other purposes.

17.3 Data Protection Technologies

Storage technologies that can be used to protect data include a disk or tape backup that copies designated information to a disk-based storage array or a tape cartridge device so it can be safely stored. Mirroring can be used to create an exact replica of a website or files so they are available from more than one place. Storage snapshots can automatically generate a set of pointers to information stored on tape or disk, enabling faster data recovery, while continuous data protection (CDP) backs up all the data in an enterprise whenever a change is made.

17.3.1 Backups: Backup has traditionally been the key to an effective data protection strategy. Data is periodically copied, typically each night, to a tape drive or tape library where it would sit until something goes wrong with the primary data storage. That is when the backup data would be accessed and used to restore lost or damaged data.

Backups are no longer a stand-alone function. Instead, they are being combined with other data protection functions to save storage space and lower costs.

Backup and archiving have been treated as two separate functions. Backup's purpose is to restore data after a failure, while an archive provides a searchable copy of data.

17.3.2 Data Portability: Data portability means the ability to move data among different application programs, computing environments or cloud services. It presents another set of problems and solutions for data protection. On the one hand, cloud-based computing makes it possible for customers to migrate data and applications between or among cloud service providers (CSP). On the other hand, it requires safeguards against data duplication.

Either way, cloud backup is becoming more prevalent.

Organizations frequently move their backup data to public clouds or clouds maintained by backup vendors. These backups can replace on-site disk and tape libraries, or they can serve as additional protected copies of data.

Another area where data protection technologies are coming together is in the merging of backup and disaster recovery (DR) capabilities. Virtualization has played a major role here, shifting the focus from copying data at a specific point in time to continuous data protection.

Traditionally, data backup has been about making duplicate copies of data. Disaster recovery, on the other hand, has focused on how backups are used once a disaster happens. Snapshots and replication have made it possible to recover much faster from a disaster than in the past. When a server fails, data from a backup array is used in place of the primary storage, but only if steps are taken to prevent that backup from being modified.

17.3.3 Data Corruption: When data is corrupted or accidentally deleted, snapshots can be used to set things right. Most storage systems today can track hundreds of snapshots without any significant effect on performance.

Storage systems using snapshots can work with key applications, such as Oracle and Microsoft SQL Server, to capture a clean copy of data while the snapshot is occurring. This approach enables frequent snapshots that can be stored for long periods of time.

When data becomes corrupted or is accidentally deleted, a snapshot can be mounted and the data copied back to the production volume, or the snapshot can replace the existing volume. With this method, minimal data is lost and recovery time is almost instantaneous.

17.4 Data Security and Data Privacy

In general, data security refers specifically to measures taken to protect the integrity of the data itself against manipulation and malware, while privacy refers to controlling access to the data. Understandably, a privacy breach can lead to data security issues.

Data privacy laws and regulations vary from country to country and even from state to state, and there is a constant stream of new ones. China's data privacy law went into effect from June 1, 2017. The European Union's General Data Protection Regulation (GDPR) went into effect in 2018. Compliance with any one set of rules is complicated and challenging.

Co-ordinating among all the disparate rules and regulations is a massive task. Being out of compliance can mean steep fines and other penalties, including having to stop doing business in the country or region covered by the law or regulation.

For a global organization, experts recommend having a data protection policy that complies with the most stringent set of rules the business faces, while, at the same time, using a security and compliance framework that covers a broad set of requirements. The basics of data protection and privacy apply across the board and include:

1. Safeguarding data.
2. Getting consent from the person whose data is being collected.
3. Identifying the regulations that apply to the organization in question and the data it collects.
4. Ensuring employees are fully trained in the nuances of data privacy and security.

17.5 Need for Data Protection Legislation

Data protection legislation is required because it can provide guidance and best practice rules for organisations to follow on how to use personal data including the following:

1. Regulating the processing of personal data.
2. Protecting the rights of the data subject.
3. Enabling the Data Protection Authority to enforce rules.
4. Holding organisations liable to fines in the event of a breach of the rules.

Rules under the legislation should be thorough and cover sharing of data, and data security. The law should provide stronger protection for more sensitive information such as:

1. Ethnic background.
2. Political opinions.
3. Religious beliefs.
4. Health.
5. Sexual life.
6. Criminal history.

17.6 European Union Data Protection Directive

EU updated its data privacy laws with a directive that went into effect May 25, 2018. The General Data Protection Regulation (GDPR) replaced the EU Data Protection Directive of 1995 and focuses on making businesses more transparent. It also expands privacy rights with respect to personal data.

The GDPR covers all EU citizens' data regardless of where the organization collecting the data is located. It also applies to all people whose data is stored within the European Union, whether or not they are EU citizens.

GDPR requirements include:

1. Barring businesses from storing or using an individual's personally identifiable information without that person's express consent.
2. Requiring companies to notify all affected people and the supervising authority within 72 hours of a data breach.
3. For businesses that process or monitor data on a large scale, having a data protection officer who is responsible for data governance and ensuring the company complies with GDPR.

Fines for not complying can be as much as €20 million or 4 percent of the previous fiscal year's worldwide turnover, depending on which is larger.

The GDPR, in Recital 1, notes that the protection of personal data is a fundamental right. However, in Recital 4, it says that this right must be balanced with other rights.

17.7 Data Protection Act, 1998 of United Kingdom

DPA, 1998 was an Act of Parliament of UK to protect personal data stored on computers or in an organised paper filing system. It was enacted to follow the European Union (EU) Data Protection Directive (1995) provisions on the protection, processing and movement of data.

Under the DPA, 1998, individuals had legal rights to control information about themselves. Most of the Act did not apply to domestic use, for example keeping a personal address book. Anyone holding personal data for other purposes was legally obliged to comply with this Act, subject to some exemptions. The Act defined eight data protection principles to ensure that information was processed lawfully.

It was superseded by Data Protection Act (DPA), 2018 on May 23, 2018. The DPA, 2018 supplements the EU General Data Protection Regulation (GDPR), which came into effect on May 25, 2018. The GDPR regulates the collection, storage, and use of personal data significantly more strictly.

17.8 Data Protection Act, 2018 of United Kingdom

DPA, 2018 controls how personal information is used by organisations, businesses or the government. It is the UK's implementation of the General Data Protection Regulation (GDPR) of EU.

Everyone responsible for using personal data has to follow strict rules called *data protection principles*. They must make sure the information is:

1. Used fairly, lawfully and transparently.
2. Used for specified, explicit purposes.
3. Used in a way that is adequate, relevant and limited to only what is necessary.
4. Accurate and, where necessary, kept up to date.
5. Kept for no longer than is necessary.
6. Handled in a way that ensures appropriate security, including protection against unlawful or unauthorised processing, access, loss, destruction or damage.

There is stronger legal protection for more sensitive information, such as:

1. Race.
2. Ethnic background.
3. Political opinions.
4. Religious beliefs.
5. Trade union membership.
6. Genetics.
7. Biometrics (where used for identification).
8. Health.
9. Sex life or orientation.

There are separate safeguards for personal data relating to criminal convictions and offences.

Under DPA, 2018, you have the right to find out what information the government and other organisations store about you. These include the right to:

1. Be informed about how your data is being used.
2. Access personal data.
3. Have incorrect data updated.
4. Have data erased.
5. Stop or restrict the processing of your data.
6. Data portability (allowing you to get and reuse your data for different services).
7. Object to how your data is processed in certain circumstances.
8. You also have rights when an organisation is using your personal data.

17.9 Customer Data Protection in India

The FinTech entities are heavily dependent on technology for each and every product they offer to their consumers. These entities may collect personal and sensitive information about the customer and become the custodians of such data. Therefore, the onus of CDP lies with these entities ranging from data preservation, confidentiality, integrity and availability of the same. The confidentiality of such custodial information should not be compromised at any cost, and for this suitable systems and processes across the data lifecycle need to be put in place by the FinTech entities.

Section 43A of the Indian Information Technology Act, 2000, provides for payment of compensation by a body corporate in case of negligence in implementing reasonable security practices and procedures in handling sensitive personal data or information resulting in wrongful loss to any person. In terms of section 72A of that Act, disclosure of information, knowingly and intentionally, without the consent of the person concerned and in breach of the lawful contract, is punishable with imprisonment for a term extending to 3 years and fine. Thus, the data protection is governed by the contractual relationship between the parties, and the parties are free to enter into contracts to determine their relationship, defining the terms of personal data and its dissemination. Nevertheless, there is a need for an exhaustive stand-alone legislation on data protection in India keeping in mind the innovations in FinTech and risk to personal data which comes to the possession of FinTech entities.

Bibliography

Bibliography

Akella, R. and R. Dossani (2001), "A Report on the Software Value Chain: The Indian Suppliers during the Downturn", Working Paper, Asia-Pacific Research Centre, Stanford University.

Arora, A. and S. Athreye (2002), "The Software Industry and India's Economics Development", *Information Economics and Policy,* 14(2), 253-273.

Arora, A., V.S. Arunachalam, J. Asundi and F. Ronald (2001), "The Indian Software Services Industry", *Research Policy*, 30(8), 1267-1287.

Athreye, S. (2003), "The Indian Software Industry and its Evolving Service Capability", Working Paper, The Open University, Walton Hall, Milton Keynes, UK.

Athreye, S. (2005), "The Indian Software Industry", in Arora and Gambardella (eds.), 'From Underdogs to Tigers', Oxford University Press: Oxford.

Balakrishnan, P. (2006), "Benign Neglect or Strategic Intent? Contested Lineage of Indian Software Industry", *Economic and Political Weekly*, Vol. 41, No. 36, September 9.

Balasubramanyam, V. and A. Balasubramanyam (2000), "The Software Cluster in Bangalore", in Dunning (ed.), 'Regions, Globalization and the Knowledge-based Economy', Oxford University Press: Oxford.

Bank for International Settlements and World Bank Group (2016), Committee on Payments and Market Infrastructures, "Payment Aspects of Financial Inclusion", April.

Bank for International Settlements (2017), Committee on Payments and Market Infrastructures, "Fast Payments: Enhancing the Speed and Availability of Retail Payments", January.

Basant, Rakesh and Brian Fikkert (1996), "The Effects of R&D, Foreign Technology Purchase, and Domestic and International Spillovers on Productivity in Indian Firms", *Review of Economics and Statistics*, 78(2), 187-200.

Bhattacharya, M. (2004), "Telecom Sector in India: Vision 2020", in 'India Vision 2020', The Report of the Committee on India Vision 2020, Planning Commission, Government of India and Background Papers, Academic Foundation: New Delhi.

Chandrasekhar C.P., Jayati Ghosh and Anamitra Roychowdhury (2006), "The Demographic Dividend and Young India's Economic Future", *Economic and Political Weekly*, Vol. 41, No. 49.

Chandrasekhar, C.P. (2006), "The Political Economy of IT-Driven Outsourcing" in Govindan Parayil (ed.), 'Political Economy and Information Capitalism in India; Digital Divide, Development Divide and Equity', Palgrave Macmillan.

Christine Lagarde (2018), "Winds of Change: The Case for New Digital Currency", Singapore Fintech Festival, November.

Committee on Digital Payments (2016), "Medium-term Recommendations to Strengthen Digital Payments Ecosystem", Government of India, Ministry of Finance, December.

Department of Information Technology (1996), "Guide to Electronics Industry in India", Department of Information Technology: New Delhi.

Dossani, R. and M. Kenney (2002), "Creating an Environment for Venture Capital in India", *World Development*, 30(2), 227-253.

Economist Intelligence Unit (2018), "Global Microscope 2018: The Enabling Environment for Financial Inclusion".

Espenshade, Thomas J. (1999), "High-End Immigrants and the Shortage of Skilled Labour", *Population Research and Policy Review*, 20, 135-141, Kluwer Academic Publisher: Netherlands.

Global Partnership for Financial Inclusion (2016), "G20 High-Level Principles for Digital Financial Inclusion".

Government of India, Ministry of Finance, "Economic Survey", (various years).

Government of India, Planning Commission, "Twelfth Five Year Plan: 2012-17".

Hasan, Rana (2002), "The Impact of Imported and Domestic Technologies on the Productivity of Firms: Panel Data Evidence from Indian Manufacturing Firms", *Journal of Development Economics*, 69(1), 23-49.

Heeks, R. (1996), "India's Software Industry: State Policy, Liberalization and Industrial Development", Sage Publications: New Delhi, Thousand Oaks, London.

Hugo, Graeme (2003), "Migration and Development: A Perspective from Asia", paper prepared for the International Organization for Migration.

Joseph, K.J. (2006), "Information Technology, Innovation System and Trade Regime in Developing Countries: India and the

ASEAN", Palgrave Macmillan: London.

Joseph, K.J. (1997), "Industry under Economic Liberalization: The Case of Indian Electronics", Sage Publications: New Delhi, Thousand Oaks, London.

Joseph, K.J. and Vinoj Abraham (2007), "Information Technology and Productivity: Evidence from India's Manufacturing Sector", Working Paper No. 389, Centre for Development Studies: Trivandrum.

Joshi, V. (1999), "India's Economic Reforms 1991-2001", South Asia Books: New Delhi.

Kamibayashi, Chieko (2006), "Current Migration of IT Engineers to Japan: Beyond Immigration Control and Cultural Barriers", in Christiane Kuptsch and Pang Eng Fong (eds.), 'Competing for Global Talent', ILO and ILLS, Geneva.

Kelkar, V., D. Chaturvedi and M. Dar (1991), "India's Information Economy: Role, Size and Scope", *Economic and Political Weekly*, September 14, 2153-2160.

Khadria, Binod (1999), "The Migration of Knowledge Workers: Second Generation Effects of India's Brain Drain", Sage Publications: New Delhi.

Khadria, Binod (2001), "Shifting Paradigms of Globalization: The Twenty-first Century Transition towards Generics in Skilled Migration from India:, *International Migration*, 39(5), special issue 1.

Kraemer, K.L. and J. Dedrick (2001), "Information Technology and Economic Development: Results and Policy Implications of Cross-Country Studies", in M. Pohjola (ed.), 'Information Technology, Productivity and Economic Growth', Oxford University Press: New Delhi.

Kripalani, M. and P. Engardio (2003), "The Rise of India", *Business Week*, December 8.

Kumar, N. and K.J. Joseph (2005), "Export of Software and Business Process Outsourcing from Developing Countries: Lessons from India", *Asia Pacific Trade and Investment Review*, 1(1), 91-108.

Lal, K. (1999), "Determinants of the Adoption of Information Technology: A Case Study of Electrical and Electronic Goods Manufacturing Firms in India", *Research Policy*, 28(7), 667-680.

Mani, S. (2005), "The Dragon vs. the Elephant: Comparative Analysis of Innovation Capability in the Telecommunications Equipment Industry in India and China", Working Paper No.

373, Centre for Development Studies: Trivandrum.

Nagaraj, R. (2004), "Fall in organized Manufacturing Employment: A Note", *Economic and Political Weekly*, July 24, 3387-3390.

NASSCOM (2006), "Study on Domestic Services (IT-ITES) Market Opportunity", National Association of Software and Science Components: New Delhi.

NASSCOM (2006), "The IT Software and Services Industry in India: Strategic Review., 2004", National Association of Software and Service Companies: New Delhi.

Nath, P. and A. Hazra (2002), "Configuration of Indian Software Industry", *Economic and Political Weekly*, 37(8), 737-743.

Panagariya, Arvind (2002), "India's Economic Reforms: What Has Been Accomplished? What Remains to be Done?", ERD Policy Brief Series, Economics and Research Department, Asian Development Bank.

Parthasarathi, A., and K. Joseph (2002), "Limits to Innovation in India's ICT Sector", *Science, Technology and Society*, 7(1), 13-50.

Parthasarthy, B. (2006), "The Political Economy of Indian Software Industry", in G. Parayil (ed.), 'Political Economy and Information Capitalism in India: Digital Divide and Equity', Palgrave Macmillan: New York.

Peterson, K. Ozili (2018), "Impact of Digital Finance on Financial Inclusion and Stability", Borsa: Istanbul, March 17.

Pohjola, M. (2001), "Information Technology and Economic Growth: A Cross country Analysis", in M. Pohjola (ed.), 'Information Technology, Productivity and Economic Growth', Oxford University Press: New York.

Raut, Lakshmi K. (1995), "R&D Spillover and Productivity Growth: Evidence from Indian Private Firms", *Journal of Development Economics*, 48(1), 1-23.

Reserve Bank of India (2019), "Report of the High-Level Committee on Deepening of Digital Payments", (Chairman: Nandan Nilekani), May.

Reserve Bank of India, "Report of the Working Group on FinTech and Digital Banking", November 2017.

Schüffel, Patrick (2016), "Taming the Beast: A Scientific Definition of Fintech", *Journal of Innovation Management.*

Sen, S. and F. Frankel (eds.) (2005), "India's Strategy of IT-led Growth", Centre for the Advanced Study of India: Philadelphia, PA.

Singh, P. and A. Pandey (2005), "Women in Call Centres",

Economic and Political Weekly, March 15.

Teigland, R., S. Siri, A. Larsson, A.M. Puertas, and C.I. Bogusz (eds.) (2018), "The Rise and Development of FinTech (Open Access): Accounts of Disruption from Sweden and Beyond", Routledge.

Upathdya, C., and R.A. Vasavi (2006), "Work, Culture, and Sociality in the Indian IT Industry: A Sociological Study", Final Report submitted to Indo-Dutch Programme for Alternatives in Development: Bangalore.

Van Loo, Rory (2018), "Making Innovation More Competitive: The Case of Fintech", *UCLA Law Review,* 65(1).

World Bank and the People's Bank of China (2018), "Towards Universal Financial Inclusion in China: Models, Challenges, and Global Lessons", February.

World Bank Group (2019), "Electronic Payments Acceptance", World Bank-NITI Aayog Roundtable, January.

World Bank Group (2018), "Payment Systems Worldwide: A Snapshot", September.

Websites

Ministry of Finance
Ministry of Communications
Ministry of Electronics and Information Technology
Reserve Bank of India
National Payments Corporation of India
NITI Aayog

Index

Index